CONSISTENTLY INCONSISTENT

RISING FROM A MONSTER'S CONTROL

BETHANY GREEN

MIRAMARE
PONTE

Published by Miramare Ponte Press
United States

Cover design by Happy Services

Library of Congress number: 2023914362

Hardback: ISBN-13: 979-8-9868633-3-7
Paperback: ISBN-13: 979-8-9868633-4-4
Ebook: ISBN-13: 979-8-9868633-5-1

For orders, please visit www.bethanygreenwriter.com

CONTENTS

AUTHOR'S NOTE

This is a work of nonfiction memoir. While I did not use any for research or quotes, there are public court documents and police records available as evidence to the two legal cases mentioned in this book. Additionally, because I am part of the story, I used my own personal memories of the events. Some supposition was necessary in writing dialogue, though the interactions are all based on real conversations and contain many direct quotes, as I recall them. I have endeavored to maintain the factual and quintessential integrity of all people and the events related herein. The conversations in the book all come from my recollections, though they are not written to represent word-for-word transcripts. Rather, I have retold them in a way that evokes the feeling and meaning of what was said and, in all instances, the essence of the dialogue is accurate. I have been faithful to my memory, but my subjects may remember things differently. I am telling my experience within the greater story, and only my experience.

Out of respect and for protective purposes, some names and identities in this memoir have been changed.

DEDICATION

This book is dedicated to all humans pushing through abuse; my fellow phoenixes rising from the ashes, above the flames, to their new and fierce selves. Some of you I know, and some of you I don't. But, let this be a reminder that you can and WILL survive, even if the years have been long and your hearts are weary.

You are loved. You are needed. You are seen.

On a personal note, this book is for my children.
R and E, you are the lights, the promises, and the gifts of my life. You are the reason I did not give up. I am thankful for who you both are and who you will be. Thank you for your love, for your strength, and, most importantly, for your forgiveness. Do not ever forget that all humans make mistakes, but the best humans learn from them and become better people in spite of them. You two will change the world with the lessons you've learned.

I am proud of you, I am thankful for you, and above all... I love you.

To Audra and Bridgette, I will never forget what you did for me in those hours I needed help the most. Thank you for going the extra mile to ensure my survival and my children's safety.

To Natalie, my sweet forever friend and the one to whom I owe 20-plus years of peace. What a gift you are; I love you.

To Marcy, my soul-sister and partner in all things writing and publishing—thank you for pushing me through the finish line. I could not have survived reliving this nightmare without you and your encouragement. I hope everyone in the world has a friend like you. You are exactly who I want to be when I grow up.

Lastly, I dedicate each and every word I have said, each and every smile I have smiled, each and every breath I have taken to... My husband.

Bradley, I love you. Thank you for picking up my shattered pieces and showing me how to make myself whole again. Thank you for being my mirror, my inspiration, and my biggest cheerleader. Thank you for reminding me that the words and beliefs I said and had about myself were simply lies I'd been fed for decades. Thank you for your gentle heart, your soft spirit, and for the belly laughs when I only knew tears.
Thank you for teaching my children what a real man is.
Thank you for trusting me with L, the best little human this broken world has to offer.

I love you in ways I only dreamed that love could be.
Thank you for being you.
Thank you for truly loving me.

PROLOGUE

IF I STARTED FROM THE BEGINNING, THERE'S NOT A CHANCE IN HELL that you would believe me. No one could be that naïve. No one could be that blind. But I was. And it's not even that I decided to go through with it all in the first place–oh, no–but I wasn't exactly forced into it either. The truth was, sure, I was desperate; I had given the world the entirety of my heart and soul and was in dire need of getting some love back. However, the lengths I would travel and the agony I'd subject my own body to in order to *be* loved would not be something I would easily recover from.

And that's just it, isn't it? That's the clichéd opening to any story of a woman's journey through an abusive relationship, right?

It's okay, though. You were curious and you wanted to know what made my story different. Maybe you've been there and you're nodding your head in agreement–victorious in your memories of getting out and moving forward with your new, self-created life. Or maybe you're sweating, clutching your hands to your chest out of fear that I'm about to write your truth–the truth you've been denying for far too long. Either way, you chose to pick this book up, you chose to buy it, and you chose to read these words knowing there was pain inside it. So, let this be your warning...

I was abused.

I went through abuse in really weird, and not so weird, ways. I was impossibly happy in thousands of moments, but only when I ignored the screaming siren in my soul that had been going off since the beginning. This will be raw and uncomfortable, but perhaps I'll make you chuckle a time or two. Don't count on it. I'm far too feisty to be funny.

Do me one favor before you dive further in, okay? Go to a mirror. Look at yourself directly in the eyes–MAKE IT UNCOMFORTABLE–and repeat the following:

I matter.

I matter.

I matter.

It makes no difference what anyone else says...

I MATTER.

There. Now that you know a major truth about *yourself*, I think you have a better understanding of something I could never grasp about *myself* and how I wound up being married to my abuser for nearly 14 years.

1

"You own everything that happened to you. Tell your stories. If people wanted you to write warmly about them, they should have behaved better."

— *ANNE LAMOTT*

WAKING UP ON JANUARY 1, 2018, I WAS NO LONGER THE SAME Bethany. I wasn't afraid. I wasn't confused. I wasn't riddled to the brim with guilt or shame. I felt powerful; I felt this sense of purpose, which was something I hadn't felt in over a decade. New Year's Eve has always left me plagued by dread for as long as I can remember because, for some reason, I have always believed that there was an immense amount of pressure laced within all the excitement of the unknown in the days ahead. That morning, though, I was overcome by a sense of decided determination, and the odd thing was, it wasn't even a choice. There was no resolution made, there was no plan in place. I simply awoke, understanding that I was infinitely more powerful than I had led myself to believe. I did not question it. I didn't even realize this new sense of *me* was even there. It was as simple as being born. I just... was.

While lying in bed, slowly becoming aware of my children's laughter coming from the living room, my husband rolled over and draped his arm over my chest. I remembered what Elizabeth Gilbert had uttered on her bathroom floor—the phrase that launched her into her exploration of self-discovery and into what would become the very memoir that spent over 187 weeks on the NYT Best Seller list:

I don't want to be married anymore.

When I first read her book, *EAT, PRAY, LOVE*, I felt her words tap into my bone marrow. I had only been married for three and a half years, and I had my 20-month-old child lying next to me in bed, rolling their favorite plastic car off my giant belly, which housed their soon-to-be little sibling. Even at that time when I first soaked in each letter of her book, I was already questioning my reasons for being married. It was the first time I recall actually being scared that I was trapped, but I didn't understand *why* I felt that way. Nonetheless, that book became my own walking daydream, and I would often find it as my source of reasons to break the Tenth Commandment.

In all honestly, Elizabeth's reasons and my reasons for not wanting to be married any longer were quite different. She explains again and again that she didn't want the life she had built and was expected to have. It was a gut-wrenching experience for her to go through, but the moment she embraced her truth, she set forth into her future. I, on the other hand, had wanted absolutely every part of the life I was living. The problem was, even that early on, it didn't feel right. But in 2018, lying in bed (I promise, I'm not always in bed!) with his arm so heavy across my chest, I just knew this would be the year.

I'd be brave.

I'd say no.

I'd endure whatever punishment he'd inevitably bestow upon me.

But... I would leave.

What's funny about the rest of that day is that I have no memory of it. It was odd that he was even there because he usually worked out of town on New Year's Eve. Being a Law Enforcement Officer for the United States Forest Service (USFS) meant he was often gone for weeks on end. My joke was that I was a single mom from the beginning of May through the end of October. It wasn't a joke, though. It really was the truth. I spent a grand total of 80 days in his presence in 2008. Funny, too, because I was pregnant for most of that time. But for some reason, he was home that New Year's Eve. And I hated it. I wanted to feel my new sense of direct strength alone. I had no clue why God was finally giving me clarity, you know, the very thing I'd been asking for, for years. But He was. And that was all I needed.

I didn't pull back right away. That was dangerous in a marriage like mine. Instead, I began to pay closer attention to the things I felt might not be so normal within the four walls of my home. I began to take note of all the times I felt shitty, but more importantly, *why* I felt shitty. Was it him? Or was it me truly being the selfish, misbehaved brat he often referred to me as? I collected evidence and stored it in each and every hidden room in my brain that no one but myself had access to. Well, no one but myself and God. I just kind of assumed if I kept my evidence behind those locked doors long enough, God would present them at my husband's final judgment.

Brutal?

Morbid?

Possibly borderline genius because, ultimately, that's what'll happen?

Perhaps. But nonetheless, that's what I began doing. It was

hard, folks. There were days early on where I'd sit and compare the life I was living to those around me, and I spent many an hour just devastated and angry. I hurt for my children. I was angry at myself for not seeing it sooner. I was withered down to bare bones, emotionally, and there was no hope for nourishment. I would see husbands encourage their wives to better themselves, and it would hurt me. I would hear husbands mention how in love with their wives they still were–never mentioning how "whipped into shape" they had them–and I would weep.

God, how many tears my pillow must have consumed.

But still, I collected my evidence. I made sure to be thorough in my investigation because I knew that when the time came for me to leave, I NEEDED my facts to be in line and for my reasonings to be sound. If I didn't, I'd surely lose my life, and my children would be raised by humans I didn't trust.

The tough part in 2018 was that he'd stopped drinking. Top rule with the super effective Ketogenic diet? Alcohol is a big no-no. Of course, my children and I were thrilled with that aspect of the diet because it meant Daddy wasn't going to be off his hinges on the nightly. But it actually just made him a more conscious and vastly more aware monster. He noticed *everything*, including the habits I'd formed as a way to cope with his drunken behaviors. He saw my teeth clenched. He realized how many times I would run to the bathroom to cry or to breathe. He *really* saw how often I was on my phone, living in my fantasy world on Pinterest. With him so aware, it was difficult to pinpoint specific issues I could use as excuses to run.

So that's where determination became the name of the game. I couldn't rely on the obvious—I had to expand my sheltered mind and understand that what I was experiencing just by being his wife... *was* abuse. My children were witnessing abuse every single day and were learning how to model themselves after that example. They were seeing how women ought to be treated, and they were seeing it all wrong. Not only did I owe it to myself to rise above the chaos in our home, but I owed it to their future friends, bosses, colleagues, partners, and future children.

Still, figuring out *how* was constantly in the back of my mind. *How* would I get out? *How* would I explain it to our children? *How* would I justify it to our church, to our friends, and to our family, who knew nothing of our life behind closed doors? *How* would I live as a single mother, with no experience, no education, no savings, and needing more health care than the average person? On top of all those *hows*, I just knew I was being exponentially transparent when I was in his presence. I am no secret keeper—in fact, I might hold the record for being the worst liar in the universe. So, it was no wonder that with every single movement I had, I was terrified he was reading my thoughts, equally devising a plan of his own to hold me captive. And that, ladies and gents, is when I realized how far his abuse had burrowed itself into my subconscious: I'd actually convinced myself that he could hear my thoughts, and *that* was the reason he would react the way he did.

See? It was *my* fault.

I remember that "Aha" moment. It wasn't me. But my response to that asinine idea was to simply... stop thinking. Which, as you will soon discover, is the ultimate goal of any abuser's ambitions.

That's right!

I. HAD. STOPPED. MY. OWN. THOUGHTS.

Sick, right? It was my personal survival technique. I did as I was told. I did not question him. I was groomed to his idea of sheer perfection. And yet, to him, I never did anything right. So, I shut off my own brain. I did my best to function normally (especially around other people), but for the most part, I would zone out. It worked until it didn't. And when it didn't, my life—and life in general as I came to understand it—changed forever.

In the following chapters, I go into some of the gruesome details that may resonate with you. Please understand that this mini confessional about being the ultimate victim of abuse has the potential to ooze with realizations for yourself.

Have you ever gotten to a place on your journey of self-discovery or on your road to healing from trauma where you just became sick at the thought that you *ever* allowed yourself to stoop so low? It happened to me almost every single day for nearly two full years after my escape. It's a kind of a "slap in the face with a giant flyswatter" type of moment. Then... you feel greasy. You might feel nauseated. You might glow red-hot and be furious. It's all normal. I promise. We have our moments, as victims, as survivors, where we recognize how damaged we once were. But that's where we also have to take a look into the moment; realizing that the mere fact that the memory bothers us or sickens us *that* much, is a tremendous gift. It means we've grown! It means we *see* the abuse. We can therefore acknowledge it and move forward.

Entering 2018 the way that I did, you must understand that I had *a lot* of growing up and learning to do. I had to research just exactly what abuse was. Believe it or not, I literally typed (through unfathomable tears) into the Google search bar, "Is it rape if it's between a husband and a wife?" The homework I'd given myself was gruesome. In and of itself, it was torture, because, again, I was itemizing each encounter and learning what was acceptable and what was crossing the line. I was tired... I was so tired. But I saw my children's faces and knew I had to keep learning.

For ease's sake, I would like to lay out the definitions of specific terms that will be used throughout this book. I feel the less research you must do while performing emotional open-heart surgery on yourself, the better. Understand that these are just a handful of terms I found from a *very* helpful and insightful website, TheHotline.org. They have an easy close-tab option and multiple ways of seeking help if you are in danger. But they helped me open my eyes to a multitude of things I was unaware of, including precise definitions of terms previously unknown to me.

TYPES AND TERMS OF ABUSE
AS DEFINED BY THEHOTLINE.ORG

PHYSICAL: You may be experiencing physical abuse if your partner has or repeatedly does any of the following abusive behaviors:

- Pulls your hair or punches, slaps, kicks, bites, chokes, or smothers you.
- Forbids or prevents you from eating or sleeping.
- Uses weapons against you, including firearms, knives, bats, or mace.
- Prevents you from contacting emergency services, including medical attention or law enforcement.
- Harms your children or pets.
- Drives recklessly or dangerously with you in the car or abandons you in unfamiliar places.
- Forces you to use drugs or alcohol, especially if you have a history of substance abuse.
- Traps you in your home or prevents you from leaving.
- Throws objects at you.
- Prevents you from taking prescribed medication or denies you necessary medical treatment.

EMOTIONAL AND VERBAL: You may be in an emotionally or verbally abusive relationship if your partner attempts to exert control by:

- Calling you names, insulting you, or constantly criticizing you.
- Acting jealous or possessive or refusing to trust you.
- Isolating you from family, friends, or other people in your life.
- Monitoring your activities with or without your knowledge, including demanding to know where you go, who you contact, and how you spend your time.
- Attempting to control what you wear, including clothes, makeup, or hairstyles.
- Humiliating you in any way, especially in front of others.
- Gaslighting you by pretending not to understand or refusing to listen to you; questioning your recollection of facts, events, or sources; trivializing your needs or feelings; or denying previous statements or promises.
- Threatening you, your children, your family, or your pets (with or without weapons).
- Damaging your belongings, including throwing objects, punching walls, kicking doors, etc.
- Blaming you for their abusive behaviors.
- Accusing you of cheating or cheating themselves and blaming you for their actions.
- Cheating on you to intentionally hurt you and threatening to cheat again to suggest that they're "better" than you.
- Telling you that you're lucky to be with them or that you'll never find someone better.

SEXUAL: You may be experiencing sexual abuse if your partner has or repeatedly does any of the following:

- Forces you to dress in a sexual way you're uncomfortable with.
- Insults you in sexual ways or calls you explicit names.
- Forces or manipulates you into having sex or performing sexual acts, especially when you're sick, tired, or physically injured from their abuse.
- Chokes you or restrains you during sex without your consent.
- Holds you down during sex without your consent.
- Hurts you with weapons or objects during sex.
- Involves other people in your sexual activities against your will.
- Ignores your feelings regarding sex.
- Forces you to watch or make pornography.
- Intentionally gives you or attempts to give you a sexually transmitted infection.

SEXUAL COERCION: Sexual coercion lies on the continuum of sexually aggressive behavior, and it may vary in practice from begging and persuasion to forced sexual contact. It may be verbal and emotional through statements made to pressure, guilt, or shame, or it may appear more subtly. Even if your partner isn't forcing you to perform sexual acts against your will, making you feel obligated to do them at all is coercion in itself.

- Implying that you owe them something sexually in exchange for previous actions, gifts, or consent.
- Giving you drugs or alcohol to "loosen up" your inhibitions.

- Using your relationship status as leverage, including by demanding sex as a way to "prove your love" or by threatening to cheat or leave.
- Reacting with sadness, anger, or resentment if you say no or don't immediately agree to something, or trying to normalize their sexual demands by saying that they "need" it.
- Continuing to pressure you after you say no or intimidating you into fearing what will happen if you say no.

FINANCIAL: This abuse can take many forms and may include:

- Providing an allowance and closely monitoring how you spend it, including demanding receipts for purchases.
- Depositing your paycheck into an account you can't access.
- Preventing you from viewing or accessing bank accounts.
- Preventing you from working, limiting the hours that you can work, getting you fired, or forcing you to work certain types of jobs.
- Maxing out your credit cards without permission, not paying credit card bills, or otherwise harming your credit score.
- Stealing money from you, your family, or your friends.
- Withdrawing money from children's savings accounts without your permission.
- Living in your home but refusing to work or contribute to the household.

- Forcing you to provide them with your tax returns or confiscating joint tax returns.
- Refusing to provide money for necessary or shared expenses like food, clothing, transportation, medical care, or medicine.

DIGITAL: Examples of digitally abusive behavior include:

- Telling you who you can or can't follow or be friends with on social media.
- Sending you negative, insulting, or threatening messages or emails.
- Using social media to track your activities.
- Insulting or humiliating you in their posts online, including posting unflattering photos or videos.
- Sending, requesting, or pressuring you to send unwanted explicit photos or videos, sexts, or otherwise compromising messages.
- Stealing or insisting on being given your account passwords.
- Constantly texting you or making you feel like you can't be separated from your phone for fear that you'll anger them.
- Looking through your phone or checking up on your pictures, texts, and phone records.
- Using any kind of technology (such as spyware or GPS in a car or phone) to monitor your activities.
- Using smart home technology, smart speakers, or security cameras to track your movements, communications, and activities.
- Creating fake social media profiles in your name and image, or using your phone or email to send

messages to others pretending to be you, as a way to embarrass or isolate you.

That's a lot to take in, I know. I hope that you're okay, having read through some definitions you maybe didn't identify as abuse before now. But believe me, precious human, it's abuse. If it doesn't feel good, and the behavior continues even after you've communicated with your partner/parent/coworker/etc., then it's time to take a harder look into what's really going on. Or... it might be time to leave.

These are all hard decisions to come to, and I'm so sorry that you're sitting there hurting all alone. Please know that I am with you—as are *many* of your fierce brothers and sisters who are ready and willing to help you get the hell out of your situation. Do not hesitate to reach out. In fact, stop reading this instant and make forward progress to getting to safety. All the phone numbers and websites that you could possibly need are in the very back of this book. Go there. Grab your phone. Get to safety. Then email me *immediately* so I can pray with and/or listen to you. I've got your back.

If you read those definitions having already survived, I know you aren't feeling so hot, either. Believe me, they were hard for me to write. Sometimes just reading a sentence or two forces you to relive a scenario you've worked extremely hard to forget. But here's the thing: you lived through it. You survived. I'm freaking proud of you, and I celebrate with you! If, however, you're already feeling the rush of pain or fear or panic, please know that I'm here for you as well. Email me. Let's talk. I absolutely mean it; we're on the same team.

If you are here having never been in a situation like mine but are reading out of love and knowledge, welcome. It's people like you who will stand up and be the voice of the voiceless. I know that if I'd had someone like you in my life, my story would be quite different.

No matter who you are, you have your reasons for holding this book in your hands. You are ready to change the game by setting out to understand a life that may or may not differ from yours. Take many deep breaths; it's time to tell my story.

2

"The problem was she wanted to be loved so badly she couldn't tell it wasn't love."

— *LEO CHRISTOPHER*

FRESH OUT OF HIGH SCHOOL, I'D ALREADY LOST A FRIEND. IT'S NOT like I'd had many to begin with, but I never saw suicide as an option for him. He was a sweet guy, too: he never said much, had a wild but supportive family, loved Metallica, and smirked whenever he saw me. I mean, he was well over six feet tall, and I stood at a grand 60 inches. I'd smirk right back at him, knowing we both had very different views of the world... literally.

His funeral, and seeing all the friends I'd once spoken to every single day come back from college or take a break from their new lives for the weekend, was jarring for me, to say the least. These were the days before Facebook, although MySpace was becoming something mentioned more often. High school was over, so we each took on the guilt of not checking in on our friend more, with one another more. I was livid because, after my second suicide attempt (which they all knew me for), no one even noticed. But I pushed those feelings down where they belonged and stayed present for everyone else. After they all went back to their lives, I decided it was time that I, too, grew up. I didn't want to wind up like Steve; I didn't want to end my life and miss out on the chances of finding happiness. I was attending classes at my local city college, saving my pennies to go on a semester (or two) abroad in London, and preparing to tour Germany, Austria, and the Czech Republic on a choir tour. I had plans, and it took losing my friend to see how important they were to me.

I should note that just a few months prior to Steve's death, I'd met this boy—well, no. To *me,* he was no boy. To me, he was a 22-year-old hunk that was just Christian enough to win over my mother and just rebel enough to piss off my father. He was every girl's dream (at least, that's what I'd told myself). The only problem with meeting Mr. Perfect was that I had a boyfriend at the time. I talked to this gentleman on the phone every day for about a week before I grew a conscience and went full radio silence. He was sweet, though, and smart, too. He was getting his degree in biology, with an emphasis on ecology. He was a wild-land firefighter with the United States Forest Service. He was really a *cowboy.* He was absolutely the exact opposite of every-thing this creative, gothic, wannabe poetess was.

And I was obsessed.

However, I'd ghosted him (a term not yet used to describe what I'd done) and purposely lost his number. I'd remembered small details about where he said he lived and whatever, but I couldn't remember his name or where I might be able to find him. We'd met at an event my best friend had invited me to, held on a random Tuesday night.

"There'll be a rock band there, and we'll listen to a short message, and then we'll all go to Denny's!"

Rock band?

A short message?

DENNY'S??

She was my best friend for a reason. Laura spoke all my love languages so fluently.

This event was held by a Christian club called Campus Crusaders for Christ (CRU), and I was more than eager to go and spend some time around "real" college people. Going to city college, I felt less-than, and it showed. Much to Laura's delight, my boyfriend couldn't go, so we arrived together and were met by a rather large crowd. We saw a friend from high school, and I —being the giant flirt I was—jumped into his arms and gave him the biggest hug. It was at that moment that I saw... *him*. Over in a dark corner was a tight gray tank top, tight Wrangler jeans, and scuffed-up black cowboy boots, all under the brim of a black cowboy hat. I couldn't see his face, but I was intrigued. I made a mental note of it and proceeded to listen to this terrible Evanescence cover band that Laura still owes me big time for having to endure.

The message *was* short, though; it was a gift I was thankful for because I was practically frothing at the mouth thinking about Denny's. Let's be honest: Denny's was *the* place to go for kids like me who didn't want to go home but couldn't afford to go anywhere else.

I sat in the booth with Laura and looked over the menu as if I didn't have the dang thing memorized when the cowboy hat walked in. I felt a lot of blood rush to my head, so I darted through the incoming crowd to the restroom to catch my breath. When I returned, my sneaky best friend had the guy sitting at our table. I approached with an awkward smile and a smart-aleck comment about the new arrival at our booth. He flashed a smile; I was no longer sure what my name was.

Some great conversation continued over the course of the following three hours. He loved his mother, his humble life, and had a *real* job with *real* plans. I'd just turned eighteen... plans were sexy to me. At the end of the night, he asked me for my number. No one had *ever* asked me for my number before, so I thought nothing of it or of my poor boyfriend sitting at home writing "thank you" cards for his mother.

I hadn't even gotten onto the highway before the guy called. I'd put him in my old brick of a Nokia phone as "Hot Cowboy," and the rush of excitement that coursed through my veins at the sight of his name on the little black and yellow screen nearly caused me to get in a car accident. We talked into the wee morning hours. He was smitten, I could tell. I was, too, but I had quite the dilemma, considering I had this boyfriend I clearly had no feelings for. So, like a champ, I ran. I ran away from both —ghosting each of them and acting like I was perfectly fine. It worked.

Thank heavens for the days of limited Internet and no social media accounts.

After Christmas and before the second semester of school started, I got the call that Steve was dead. I went back to CRU at Fresno State and shared my story about my friend. I was prayed over but didn't really find what I was looking for that night. I was looking for *him*. He wasn't there. Why would he be? Did I even deserve the option to explain to him what had happened? I vowed to myself and Laura that I would go to this club one more Tuesday. If the cowboy was there, that was it. If he wasn't, that was the answer I needed.

The following week, I was writhing with nerves. Laura and I rode with another friend and walked onto campus arm in arm, with yours truly in the middle. They knew of my plan. They knew this would be the game changer for me, one way or another.

We walked up to the building where the meeting was, and boom. He was standing there. His arms were crossed, almost defensively, as he spoke to an interesting girl who was clearly drooling at the idea that he was even conversing with her. With utmost bravery, I broke through the crowd of CRU members and walked directly up to him. Interrupting the poor girl, I said, "I need to speak with you." I turned around and walked out the double doors, past Laura and a group of loud theater geeks reciting lines from West Side Story. I was thrilled when I looked over my shoulder and he was following me. When I got him alone, I looked him directly in the eyes and apologized for ignoring him those months ago. I begged to please be given a second chance. His eyebrows were so high at the brim of his forehead that I thought they might shoot off his face. He told me he thought I was rude, but if I promised not to do it again, we could try. He grabbed my hand and kissed it... like a gentleman.

And that was it.

I felt like I'd grown up and was officially looking at my future. I'd made it. My fairytale was beginning.

Now... knowing where this is all going, are you seeing the red flags yet? Are you seeing how I bowed before a man I didn't know *at all* and apologized for something I had absolutely no reason to be sorry about? Sure, one can be sorry for *how* things played out, but I didn't need to be sorry and beg for a second chance. And then to promise not to do it again? No. What I did at that moment was fork over ownership of myself. You and I can sit here and rationally think, *How can you promise THAT? You don't even know what his name is!* But that narrative didn't fall into the fairytale my mind craved. His demand was romantic, and that is all I allowed myself to see.

FROM THAT MOMENT ON, he and I were inseparable. Of course, we were. His dreams were addicting, and I wanted to be part of them. After one week, he told me he loved me. It didn't matter to me that it was on the same day that he screamed at me for chuckling a little bit when he was semi-frustrated about traffic. The fact that he got into my face and shouted, "You will NEVER do that again! What are you, 15? If you're going to be mine, you will learn to NEVER laugh at me. It's immature, and I won't have it!" didn't faze me, because, after all, he *loved* me. And in real love, as he explained it, people fight. "It's when they stop fighting that you have to worry," he'd said.

Knowing the Bible stories, I imagined how Eve must have felt when the serpent spoke to her. Was he as intoxicating? Were Satan's words dripping with temptation the way this cowboy's words were for me? I understood Eve's plight. But in those moments, I wouldn't dare compare her situation to mine. After all, she was doing something against God. God was clearly leading me... right? Those two renderings couldn't at all be reversed, could they?

By the third month of dating, I'd called off my semester(s) studying in London. How could I abandon the man I loved? It was bad enough when I was gone to Germany, Austria, and the Czech Republic for two weeks. I wrote to him every single day, missing out on once-in-a-lifetime excursions in order to show my devotion. I even paid for a *very* expensive phone call on his birthday, where everyone I'd coerced into coming and singing "Happy Birthday" in a true, eight-piece choral ensemble heard him *scream* at me because he hadn't heard my voice until that day. So, there was no way London could happen. It didn't matter that I'd dreamed of living that life since I was 13. He mattered. My cowboy had all the right answers.

By the fourth month, we were engaged.

I refused to listen to every concerned voice who asked all the right questions. I forged ahead. I was 18. I wanted my fairytale. My parents married at 20, so being 19 when I walked down the aisle was only a win in my book.

But that's when the isolation truly began. I wasn't allowed to see my friends without him, if at all. I wasn't allowed to invite my brother over to our little mobile home that my then-fiancé rented for us. And I was no longer able to go to school. I wasn't too disappointed about that rule, though. I wasn't much for school, and I found the decision to be in my best interest at the time. However, all the other things were of major importance to me. "*We* are each other's friends now. *I* don't have friends other than you. My parents have been married almost 30 years, and they've *never* had friends. You aren't in high school anymore, so you don't need to prance around town without me."

Our arguments were also more constant than one could rationally conceive. I was never right; I was always too lippy and disrespectful. I had been kicked out of the car in various locations a multitude of times when we were arguing in the car. I chalked it up to what *real* love was like, and I always believed him when he assured me that *I* was the one who had growing up to do.

When the day of our wedding came, nothing went right. I'd planned my wedding out since I was five years old; I knew the way it was supposed to feel. I had always dreamed of getting married in late October, barefoot in a forest somewhere. I didn't want anyone to sit in chairs because I didn't want to disturb the earth. I wanted words and poems and vows that reflected our hearts. I wanted dark colors; I wanted something hauntingly beautiful, old-worldly, and deeply rooted in the passion my soon-to-be husband and I had for one another. And the reception? Oh, I wanted it to be a PARTY, celebrating not only the beautiful day we'd all had together but the future as well.

Instead, we married in the middle of March, at a restaurant/clubhouse that meant nothing to me, and not only was I not barefoot... I was wearing antique cowgirl boots. My brother was two hours late, and I could tell he, without a doubt, did *not* want to be there. My parents were fighting; my father was not wearing his wedding ring. As the number one believer in my parents' fairytale, I was crushed and couldn't even allow myself five minutes to process what that symbol (or lack thereof) meant. My about-to-be mother-in-law wore the same outfit and grim scowl she'd worn the week prior when my almost-brother-in-law married *his* child bride in a soul-crushing wedding of their own. (Yes, they married one week to the day before we did. That's another fun tale.)

We had *literal* shotguns at our ceremony, and my pretentious family was so awkward about the whole ordeal that it was unbearable. And then, if all those omens weren't enough, I sliced my finger wide open ten whole minutes before I was to pledge my life to this monstrosity. Looking back, everything was telling me to run. But I was/am a stubborn, stubborn girl. I wanted to prove everyone wrong.

I wish I hadn't silenced my spirit.

At 4:00 p.m. on that extra hot day in March, I became a Mrs. I was 19. I was broken. But I forced myself to believe I was finally free. My emotions were so caught up in escaping my childhood, which was wrought with misery on its own, that I didn't see— truly see—how terrifying and complicated my life would become.

Before our honeymoon was over, we had gotten into three *major* fights—I discovered he had a chewing tobacco habit that I knew nothing of, *and* I was accused of aligning my birth control incorrectly so that I'd be on my period during our week-long stay in Colorado Springs, just to rob him of his rites/rights.

The very first time I thought *It shouldn't be this hard* was when we were fighting in our rental car on our way to sightsee in Denver. I wasn't exactly referring to the fact that it was snow- ing, that we'd planned our entire honeymoon around the cowboy/Western lifestyle he loved—even though all the touristy stuff wasn't open in the off-season—or the fact that he wouldn't stop freaking out over money. No, I was referring to how hard I was already fighting to make sense of why this human was viewing life and treating his new bride the way he was. It was a thought that repeated itself over and over, to the point where you will soon discover how brainwashed I truly became.

That whole first year of our marriage was a struggle in many ways. I helped him through school, working two jobs for a while. I adjusted to doing all the housework, all the cooking, all the serving, all the laundry, and all the submitting to him pretty quickly. I figured out that the less I argued, the less I stood up for myself, the fewer times we fought. I struggled the most with his family and their sheer hatred of me. To them, I was a "city girl" whose ideas were ridiculous, self-righteous, and snotty. When I spent my first ever Thanksgiving away from my parents (who were divorcing at the time and had decided not to have a Thanksgiving dinner) that first year, his mother laughed at me and said I was "such a little girl" and asked, "Why are you crying? It's just dinner."

The signs were there, right?

Why couldn't I see them?

In all honesty, writing this whole chapter makes me wonder how I didn't just run the first time he kicked me out of the car in the rain, in the middle of nowhere on a cold February night. But I didn't. Instead, I forced myself to believe this was normal.

Nine months into our marriage, I wrote this journal entry:

Nope. Now that finals are over, all we have done is fight. He just left the house without saying he loves me (he went to physical therapy) or even a simple "goodbye." All because I'm wearing... not a revealing outfit, oh, no. But MAKEUP!

I swear, I'm not even wearing hardly anything! Especially not as much as I usually wear/have worn when I go out! I'm wearing foundation (because I'm embarrassed of my super red complexion) and mascara. I was just getting rid of my oily eyelids when he FLIPPED OUT. I wasn't even adding color! I was putting a neutral powder on, so my eyelids didn't look so gross! Now ALL OF A SUDDEN, I can't wear makeup... apparently it attracts attention. Just when I thought my ugly self-image couldn't be lower, now I'm being required to walk around REALLY hating the way I look. Not even slightly confident...

...Am I supposed to be married and hate myself, too? And just be happy with the fact that "at least I got married?" When can I just be myself?

WHY CAN'T HE SEE HOW MUCH HE HURTS ME?!

I guess I just have to let myself go.

ALL RIGHT, friends. Let me have it. I can take it, I promise, because I see it, too. To be fair, that argument ended with him telling me he was an idiot and that he needed to figure out how to adjust to being home after each semester ended. In a backward way, it was still my fault because I wasn't helping him adjust correctly. But, "You'll get better at this," was whispered to me before I fell asleep.

And that was the foundation of our marriage. I was attacked, we'd fight for hours, I'd cry, then he'd release his talons. After all the threats, name-calling, gaslighting, and crazy-making, he'd admit that *he* had a problem (usually with his mother) and I wasn't helping him the right way.

So... year one of marriage was in the books. He spent half of it in school and the other half fighting fires–away from home for a couple of weeks at a time–all over the western United States. I spent my time learning how to perfect hating myself, follow life according to my husband's plan, and realizing I'd made a diffi-cult choice. I wrote time and time again in my journal how much I'd changed for him and how much I missed going to poetry slams and the theater.

"God only gives us what we can handle!" Right? Lies. God warned me. God gave me plenty of opportunities. But I didn't listen. I chose to see the good. I chose to believe God was testing me. Was He? I don't believe so. I believe in the free will we are told He so lovingly trusts us with. I grew up being told, *"When we choose not to follow the right/best direction, He helps us along the way, answering our cries for help by giving us more opportunities to correct our mistakes."*

But I didn't.

Instead, I got pregnant.

3

"On the verge of tears, she smiled. That's the strongest thing I've ever witnessed."

— *R.H. SIN*

HE TOLD ME HE REALLY WANTED TO BE A FATHER.

He had repeatedly mentioned trying to have a baby around six months into our marriage, but I was uneasy about the idea. With all the turmoil I felt in my soul, I wasn't sure I was ready. I was overweight, and my Type-1 Diabetes hadn't been in check for some time. Plus, I was questioning that small, random whisper I'd hear over my heart:

It shouldn't be this hard.

After our first anniversary and a move to a new place, it was fire season again. He was gone all of the time because it was a particularly scorching summer in the midst of a rainless year in the west. I had time to think. I had a job that I loved, working with kids with special needs. However, as time went on, what I can only describe as my biological clock started ticking. I felt pressure to compete with my brother-in-law and his wife to be the first to bring a grandchild into the family. I felt like if I could do that, they'd finally love and respect me as a daughter and sister. I'd secure my spot in the family tree because my vows, devotion, and consistency meant nothing to them.

I went to my childhood endocrinologist to get a better grasp on what it meant to be a Type-1 Diabetic as an adult. I'd lived with Juvenile Diabetes for ten years but had never taken great control of it. My doctor told me there was no way I could conceive with how crazy my blood sugar had been. I was thrilled, then sad, then relieved, then angry. My husband was gone on an assignment, so I didn't have to see his face when I told him the news.

We made a plan to go to a major theme park when he returned. He wasn't happy once I explained why getting pregnant would be a little more difficult than we'd thought, but he committed to helping me pursue the right track to losing weight and getting healthy.

The day he came home, I felt like someone had dragged me through 17 miles of dirt and rocks. I felt greasy and just really not normal. I called a good friend (the only one he allowed me to have because her husband was *his* closest friend). She told me to take a pregnancy test. I was buying them in packs of three because it saved money driving to the store all the time. At that point, I'd taken so many tests that I was beginning to dream about peeing on random things. I reluctantly did what I had to do on the stick and walked away. I knew it was negative. I grabbed laundry to put into the washer to prep for our road trip, and after a few minutes, I went back to throw away the soaked stick of disappointment.

Two lines.

Not even faint. Just... there.

I called my friend back. I screamed. I felt dizzy. I cried. She told me she was coming right over.

She showed up at my front door with two big Gatorades and three more tests of varying types. She was about six months along with her second baby, so to think we'd be pregnant together for a bit was already a perk hitting our brains.

Tests one through three all came back with immediate positives.

I was indeed pregnant.

I didn't call him; instead, I waited for him to walk through the door to share the news. I was elated. I was freaking out. I thought I might be carrying my personal savior, but I refused to acknowledge that idea. I wrapped up a bunch of little things I'd gotten him while he was gone. I often bought things—tiny things—for him. It was proof that I thought of him and him alone while he was away. I never got stuff for myself. That would be selfish.

He wasn't in the best mood when he walked in the door. Disappointing for sure. But I made him sit down anyway, enticing him with all the wrapped-up goodies. New underwear, new razors, a CD (which he got mad at me for because it was expensive), and then... the positive test.

He looked at it, and the biggest wave of fear I'd ever seen overtake a human washed completely over him. My intuition shouted the truth at me: He didn't *actually* want to be a father. He wanted to make sure I couldn't leave. I pushed that thought out of my mind so fast. After the wave of fear went hidden, his eyes hit mine. "Really?! Are you serious?"

We hugged. It was a sweet moment on the surface.

We went to tell his parents, and they barely flinched. "Oh, cool..." his father said. His father was blind (due to lack of self-care, as he was not born that way), but I'd expected at least a smile. His mother, being the ray of sunshine she was, said, "Really? That's cool. What are you gonna name it?" His brother had nothing to say, but his sister-in-law walked out of the room in tears. I won't lie; I was furious. And then I was vindicated because, clearly, I'd had the right idea about the silent competition brewing between us over who'd get pregnant first.

A *huge* family fight ensued over those moments for years on end. And I mean it; for *years,* it was brought up as a point of contention.

My husband seemed content, though. I could see the normal "new-dad" fears flash across his face occasionally, but for the most part, something appeared to settle in him a bit.

"Oh, Bethany," I hear you saying. *"You are a silly, silly girl."*

You are not wrong.

Not too long after I found out I was pregnant, I discovered a bill for over $100 that he'd spent on pornography. He purchased it the day after I told him about the baby and spent the following three days buying more and watching it while I was at work. Remember, these were the days before easily accessible Internet (plus where we lived—isolated in a small foothill community—barely got cell service). Now, some might laugh that I was so devastated over finding porn. *"Men do that, Bethany,"* you might say. Which, ew, let's not be so demeaning and sexist, shall we?

But for me, it was a massive trigger. I was told that my entire childhood and upbringing were destroyed by my father's addiction to porn. My parents were in the middle of a devastating divorce, and my mother explained to me often that she discovered my father's porn habit when she was pregnant with me. She said how she should have run and never looked back because year after year, promise after promise, she'd find him more immersed in that realm than in her. Now, while I have my own beliefs and views on the issue, they do *not* have to be yours. Personally, I feel that if your partner is hiding *anything* from you or feeling the need to have a separate life without your knowledge, they're being unfaithful to the life you two are building or have built, even if that's with food! I believe that if you aren't willing to share, do, or be something with your partner, you need to give them the courtesy to let go.

But I digress.

He spent a lot of money that we didn't have on his addiction while I was spending eight-plus hours on my feet and vomiting in trash cans and sinks while I was at work (my morning sickness was so convenient that way).

Why? He had a wife who was newly carrying *his* child. He told me he was stressed about the changes. I almost left. I packed a bag and everything. But he talked me off my ledge and promised he'd not do it again. Then I caught him hiding beer. And then tobacco. And then he upped his drinking and would get drunk instead of doing schoolwork... instead of just talking to me. There were so many lies in the shortest amount of time, so many things he was hiding before I could catch my breath, and so many excuses before I realized it was a game to him. He knew how to tug at my heartstrings because he reeled me in with the "I'm so broken and need your help" line.

Folks, I shine the brightest when I can help someone else, and he figured that out quickly.

We fought throughout the whole pregnancy. All roads led to each argument being my fault. I'd apologize, and we'd start over. I was young, after all. I had lessons to learn and maturing to do. I needed to understand that the world, *our* world, was something I needed to get used to.

Other than that, and making me continue to do all the housework, go to all my doctor's appointments alone, and him drinking all the time, my pregnancy went okay. I was so lonely. I couldn't wait to have my tiny human with me to keep me occupied and give me a reason to keep breathing. In the end, I was beyond stressed. My doctor diagnosed me with Pruritic Urticarial Papules and Plaques of Pregnancy (PUPPP), which meant I was having a reaction that caused every square inch of my swelling body to itch. I wasn't sleeping whatsoever and was always alone. It felt like my body was giving up, but my heart and mind refused.

Our first child was born one week to the day after our second wedding anniversary. They were just shy of a month early. I nearly lost my life and theirs. After an emergency cesarean, our 5lb 13oz bundle of perfection solidified my existence on this planet. I felt I had a purpose for the first time in my meager 21 years.

My husband was proud. He boasted about his accomplishment to everyone.

Hours after our child's arrival, my husband abruptly left for school, claiming he had a class that was mandatory to attend. He explained that his professor wouldn't give him a pass for missing the quiz that night just because of having a child. I called him out for lying, but he swore he had to go. I spent most of my first night as a new mom alone in the hospital. I didn't hate it, but I was furious that he put yet another thing in front of us.

Until that point, I was used to being told I didn't do things right: I didn't communicate correctly, I wasn't enough of a country girl, I didn't keep the house clean enough, and I most certainly didn't satisfy him in the bedroom. I was used to being controlled in every aspect of my life, but having a child, I had what I considered to be the biggest bargaining chip. I had control over something he couldn't and wouldn't dare have control over.

You see, coming home and adjusting to life as a new family of three is hard for anyone. But not him. It was easy. He'd claimed when we were dating that he'd never change a diaper because that was the woman's job. When I say he held on to that resolve, I mean it. The nurses had him change our child's first diaper in the hospital (I was "busy" being sewn back into place), and he never let me forget it. So, life at home didn't change much for him.

On the other hand, I was a mess. I never slept because I was expected to continue to uphold my wifely duties when the baby slept. As if I hadn't been already, I was getting compared to his mother around every corner. His mother did it all and never made a single mistake or complained once. She was the gold standard for all women to hold themselves to, and I could NOT win. But I figured out quickly that although I despised him for not lifting a finger to help me, I actually made it my personal mission not to *need* the help. This way, I could control what happened with our baby. I made sure my husband knew nothing about what it meant to raise a child so that I wouldn't be lying when I told people he didn't know how. I wouldn't be lying.

Strange how you justify chaos when you're drowning in it, eh?

A couple of rage-filled months later, he graduated with his degree. Then, boom—it was fire season again, but this time, he'd been promoted. The chip on his shoulder certainly began to form and form fast. His constant stress about not getting enough overtime, about when he'd have to start paying his student loans, and about getting accepted into the Law Enforcement Academy was unbelievable. Seeing our child's face wasn't enough to keep the monster from occasionally baring its teeth. In fact, my husband resented our tiny bundle of joy. He couldn't handle—and I swear he said this—that he had to share my body with a baby. I was *his,* and he just wanted to give our child solid food as soon as it was allowed. He mentioned more times than not that he was jealous of our 3-month-old.

Life became even harder when his focus shifted to the Federal Law Enforcement Academy. He rarely ate, was always working out, and often did not come home from work until he'd gotten another round of exercise in. I understood his goal: he wanted to be in the best shape possible for the Academy. He knew his dreams were at stake, but at what cost?

He did start to focus more of his attention on the baby and me. My journal entries lit up with exclamations like "Finally!" and "It's been so wonderful!" and "We actually talked it out!" And once he got his assignment and Academy date, he buckled down on the family man routine. Our child's first Christmas was beautiful.

Like any rational person, I believed that perhaps I was getting a glimpse of my happy future. Maybe I had earned the right to smile after all the hell I had been through helping him through school and taking the brunt of his frustrations.

Federal Law Enforcement Training Center (FLETC) was located across the country, and he was set to be gone for 16 straight weeks. When he was gone, he missed our third anniversary, our baby's first steps, first haircut, and first birthday. I'd gotten into an awful accident that totaled my car. I had to begin packing up our house for our relocation. It was madness. And he didn't trust me one bit. His tone changed as we spoke on the phone each night. I constantly spoke of how proud of him I was and kept up the front he'd asked me to show when it came to my emotions. He told me he couldn't handle *both* his stress and mine, so mine wasn't important.

Friends and family scraped the money to buy my plane ticket for his graduation. He was actually excited to see us when we got there. Our kiddo walked to him, and the ultra-skinny stranger, who I barely recognized as my husband, actually cried as he held his little one. It was a moment I'll never forget.

Bliss couldn't even come close to what it felt like being together again. Sure, an adjustment had to happen—a lot changes in a baby's life in just four months. We had a welcome home/birthday celebration for him, which I felt was important because he hadn't seen his family and deserved to be celebrated.

I wasn't feeling well, so I caught incredible grief from his parents and eventually from him.

Keep in mind, the entire four months he was gone, his parents saw their grandson and me *twice*. That might not be the biggest deal in the world, except that they lived about 1,200 yards away from us. Still, I was feeling greasy and gross. As we solidified where we were moving, started collecting boxes, and began packing up, I just felt worse and worse.

I remembered I'd felt that way once before...

Sure enough, baby number two made its presence known.

My husband was less than thrilled this time. I kept it secret once again but wrote "Big [Sibling]" on our child's shirt and had them meet their daddy at the front door when he got home from work.

This time, I had a video camera to capture the moment.

"Hey, kid! What's that written on your shirt? It says BIG... no way. Turn off the camera. TURN. IT. OFF."

It shouldn't be this hard.

We moved, and he was gone again. He had three trainings to do, and he was gone six weeks each time. The dates were not guaranteed, nor were the locations. Because he was Federal, anywhere with a National Forest could call him for training. The first place called pretty quickly. He went to Kentucky and was gone for six weeks. He missed hearing our unborn child's heartbeat for the first time, my birthday, and our firstborn hitting milestone after milestone. He refused to let me be emotional. He said I needed to "woman up" because military wives have it so much worse.

He's absolutely right—they sure do. I will never say they don't. Let's make that clear. They have bigger balls than most men I know, enduring a life where they often come second to their spouse's occupation. But they, too, have feelings. And their idea of "toughness" might be wholly different from his assumptions.

Many traumatic things happened while he was gone on that assignment, including my dog killing a neighbor's goat, my mother slipping further into her prescription pill addiction, a massive mouse infestation in the country home we'd just moved into, and our child seemed to have a medical concern that needed immediate attention and minor surgery. Considering my husband was not there, I was in my second trimester of pregnancy *and* had no support system because he'd isolated me for so long that I had no one to call for help; I wondered what God's plans were. My husband had me trained that I was not to go out unless I needed groceries or essentials. I was so, so very lonely.

He went on his other two assignments almost immediately after he came home. That year, I saw him a grand total of 80 days out of 366 (it was a Leap Year). Christmas came and went, and we moved a second time—this time, to one of the most isolated places I've ever lived in. There was no Internet and no cell service. I had a house phone, but that was my only link to the outside world. I was eight months along, and the closest hospital was over an hour and a half away. I loved the house at least, so I made sure to nest abundantly in the time I had left before our new baby was born. My husband was thrilled. We were only a few miles from his duty station, and his ability to keep the outside world away from his wife (or was it the other way around?) was secure.

Our second miracle arrived a month later. They were born via elected cesarean because we wanted to get my tubes tied. And, of course, by "we" I mean *he*. I remember being in the doctor's office by myself when my doctor came in with the paperwork. I was 35 weeks pregnant. She said, "Now, Bethany, normally, we don't suggest getting a tubal ligation at your age. But your husband is all but demanding it, and well, you *are* a

Type-1 Diabetic. Sign here. This is the official permission to sterilize you."

I was 23.

After she left the room, I burst into tears. I didn't necessarily *want* more children, but the thought that the option was being taken away from me at such a young age broke my heart. But I didn't have a choice. My husband didn't want more mouths to feed, and considering that despite being 2009, we still lived in a misogynistically-inclined society, I wasn't allowed to govern or make choices for my own body.

In the hospital, after our beautiful towheaded second child was born, I was devastated and suicidal. Though they were full-term, they were sick with something the doctors couldn't quite figure out. The doctor informed me that the fluid in their lungs hadn't been pushed out due to not going through the birth canal (*thanks for making my guilt and brokenness so much worse, Doc*), so they had to stay in the nursery for the first 24 hours of their life. I wasn't able to see nor touch my baby until they were about 9 hours old. My hormones and emotions were through the roof. Then, my husband had to leave to take care of our firstborn. We had no support (other than my husband's grandmother and aunt, who watched our kiddo the night before their sibling was born). I spent my first night postpartum with no husband, no family, and, worst of all... no baby.

I was a wreck.

I endured month after month of postpartum depression. I had no outlet, no one to see, no one to watch my children while I took care of myself. And when summer arrived, I found that it was so much worse than fire season because my husband was not only gone for weeks at a time, but he'd also developed such an arrogant, self-entitled attitude that I'd lost the remaining parts of who I pretended he was to begin with.

He spent most of his time cleaning up illegal marijuana

groves on Federal land. He'd "short-haul" (laymen's terms: a 30-minute to 3-hour helicopter ride, hanging from a line roughly 30 feet under the belly of the machine) into these groves, which was extremely dangerous on its own, and then he'd rid the mountainside of the illegal aliens and illegal plants. The amount of precise organization it took for these things to happen was no less than what it takes to plan a secret military operative. The government was very serious about these things, and my husband ate his status up. He felt powerful pulling people over, finding all the ways they were wrong, and arresting them. He proudly carried his gun *everywhere* he went, claiming the world was not safe.

His ego soared.

After a year of living in complete isolation, his desire to become better than his parents and brother overtook his soul. He didn't want the small, country lifestyle any longer. He'd almost made it his personal goal to make them feel inferior when he was around. We searched for a couple of months and bought a house in the city. It wasn't exactly a small place, and it wasn't exactly something I hated after years of living in trailers and taking care of large amounts of unused property. Tension grew each time we were around his family, though; the only one they blamed was me.

I'd lost the ability to care about their insurmountable hatred, especially since it was clear my husband got off on ruffling their feathers. Besides, I was elated to finally be around human beings! He permitted me to take short trips to Target, parks with the kids, the grocery store (when he couldn't make it), and church alone. I *did* have to text him when I left and when I arrived anywhere I went, but it didn't faze me. Each outing was the opportunity to be part of the world again.

It's funny, though, that's about as good as it got. The excitement was replaced with financial fears and the need to keep up appearances.

It shouldn't be this hard.

I remember a whole lot of darkness freckled with spots of genuine and pure moments. My husband was working 10-to-12-hour days and complained the entire time he had to take a day off. I was still alone, but this time with two babies under the age of four all day, every day. I lived and breathed by them. With them, I could keep pushing. I often caught myself smiling because the days ahead seemed manageable. Maybe it was just a matter of abandoning our country-living ideals. I could put up with the new direction we were navigating.

Or so I thought.

4

_____

"It's not your fault. Sometimes, brave women fall in love with cowards."

— R.H. SIN

WE WERE AN OFFICIAL ALL-AMERICAN FAMILY. WE HAD purchased our first home, had two beautiful children, two dogs, I was a stay-at-home mother, and he... took care of us all. We'd accomplished all of this before either one of us had seen our 30th birthday. We lived in a cookie-cutter neighborhood where all the houses, cars, and women looked the same.

I was ecstatic.

I hated the thought of living in a place like that, but I had been so horrifically isolated, that I was willing to overlook many of the things that I once thought were a death sentence. I was proud of our house and the status it felt like we'd achieved. I found that I became everything I hated in a person: judgmental and haughty, with a slight hint of elitist entitlement. I'd decided to match my husband's arrogance because it meant I was not only not fighting with him as much, but I also no longer had to fight with myself. I allowed my former self to die officially. I'd forgotten my love for poetry, my love for Halloween, my love for people. I hardened my heart in many ways behind closed doors. What choice did I have? I was stuck with no hope for the life I'd dreamed about. Instead, I was given pieces of what I wanted, just in different forms.

I poured myself into my kids. And when I say poured, I mean it. We went on walks, we went to the park, we got Slurpees at Target, we adventured to splash pads and the mall. I had "Four-Wallers," as my husband called it, meaning I was tired of being in the house. I took them on playdates with a friend he approved of who had two young kids of her own. It felt like I had a life.

I also finally had Internet. I was a *real* person! He allowed me to go through a writing course I'd heard of through a parenting magazine; I was obsessed. It gave me a bit of a hobby and allowed me to have something of my own. If I wrote a book that sold, he said that would be great extra income for our family (are all you writers laughing a little or a whole lot right now?). Because of this, he also allowed me to have a Facebook account to begin connecting with other writers. I liken that permission to how it must feel when a kidnapper allows his abductee to see some sunlight after being in a basement for five years. I got to talk to people! I got to "see" friends and family with whom I'd lost contact after I'd met him.

He monitored a lot of what I did, who I interacted with, and he had to approve of all friend requests—especially if they were men.

"He's my math teacher from 8th grade. He's in his sixties, is married, and is no threat."

"Yes, I knew him from high school, but we didn't date. He's gay."

"He's from church."

These were just a few of the over-explanations I had to give when showing him the profiles of the men I had to ask permission to accept friend requests. There were plenty of times he'd become so irate when scouring through my friends list, screaming that I would cheat on him. The accusations became a daily conversation. The hilarious truth was that I could no more imagine cheating on him than I could imagine being happy any longer.

There was no desire to be with anyone if all men were like him.

As HAPPY AS I was having a new life and exploring my smaller bouts of freedom, things began to wilt in our household. Like the most clichéd frog in a pot of slow-boiling water, it took me a year to realize things were... *changing*. Soon, the insufferable desire to cut myself like I did in my teens returned. The fear of him coming home every night got worse each day. This is a little humorous to me now because, looking back to that point in our relationship, I wouldn't even deem him scary. I'd seen nothing yet—at least not in reality.

My dreams were flooded with premonitions of exponential horror. Still, I kept putting my best smile on and stepping one foot in front of the other for the sake of my children. It got to a place where my husband and I were barely speaking. Sex, to him, was the only way to verify that we "were okay," and we were hardly doing that anymore. He was drinking a lot more and working even more than that, and I had no fight to have conversations about it. I was thrilled not to have to fake something else in my day for a while.

Someone once asked me if there was ever a point where I could have left him without too much pain. I guess the truth is, this might have been a safe time. However, even though I was miserable, divorce was *not* an option. My Pentecostal parents raised me to believe divorce was only okay if a spouse was unfaithful or physically abusive. My mother often told me, "Bethany, if a man—especially your husband—ever hits you, run. RUN. Do not look back. He does it once; he will do it again. Do *not* forget this." So that's the only thing I understood abuse to be.

My thoughts were scattered after a few months of living in the downward spiral that was my marriage. I kept reaching out to him but was rejected at all points. The further we drifted, the deeper my confusion and fear dove. Was he having an affair? That might be convenient, but not likely. I began to panic. If we split up, I knew what that would mean for me. I would be left with nothing. I had no job, no education, no money of my own. The house, our truck, everything was all only in his name. I see now how strategic he was and that I'd allowed it to happen because I would have had nothing if I didn't. I made the hasty decision to put bandages over every gaping, gushing wound in our life. I am not a quitter. I blamed myself for the slump we were in—of course, I did—I'd been trained to—and sought answers to fix what was clearly breaking.

Sex was his muse. It was involved in every way he ever tried to show love. It was the point of any relationship, he said; it was definitely the basis of ours. Without it, he felt betrayed. He hated being gone from home, not because he missed his family, per se, but because his balls would hurt. And he didn't like that. It made him insane and angry, and he never hesitated to make sure I knew that. When he'd get home from long assignments or work-days, I knew where my place was. Because I could tell our relationship was falling apart, I did the one thing I would regret for the rest of my life.

I read a book.

But not just any book. I read a book (plus its sequels, immediately thereafter) that became a worldwide phenomenon, topping the NYT Best Seller lists for weeks, leading to three box office hits. The series featured a young, impressionable girl who falls for a very rich, attractive young man who turns out to be into a lifestyle the girl had never heard of. Before too long, she becomes his submissive, and he her Dom. Because of this popular book series, the inner workings of the BDSM, D/s lifestyle had become something that "regular" people openly talked about. The jokes were endless. The books were terribly written, and as a writer and editor, I found that to be awfully distracting. As the stories hailing from those who had read the book(s) continued, I understood the draw and excitement for the women who were bored at home, living a mundane life. There was passion, a man taking control, and sex... a lot of wild, uninhibited, no-children-screaming-in-the-other-room sex.

But I... I read for research, believing it might have been the key to winning my husband's favor. I figured researching in the fantasy world of a book would get me in less trouble with him than if he discovered anything on my computer. I was attracted to the male character because I felt he was fair. I felt like my consistently inconsistent husband lacked direction in what he wanted from me. I felt like if he had direction, and I knew what was expected of me on a day-to-day basis, we'd fight less often, and I could lead a more normal life.

I read and read while he was gone to training for ten days. When he came home, I was set to leave for my first-ever writer's conference. He was allowing me to go because he knew the demographic of the children's book writer community was mostly made up of women. I would be staying with two women from my critique group, just for one overnight. He wasn't thrilled, but he let me go. Because I was scared my leaving would be thrown back in my face during a future argument, and in order to show my devotion to him, I showed him the books. I explained my reasonings for wanting to read them. I explained that I could tell this lifestyle was something he was wanting, and perhaps we could give it a try. I told him I wanted to make our relationship work and that I was noticing how I wasn't quite enough for him anymore. He listened intently, which was not really his style. When I finished (and yes, I was in tears, afraid of his anger), he nodded.

"Let me get this straight—you *want* to obey me? You *want* to have things demanded from you? This is really something you actually think you can do?"

Inside my head, I was screaming. Of course, it wasn't what I wanted, but I'd lost sight of my hopes and dreams eons ago. I knew that this was my only chance.

"Yes," I whispered, my eyes welling up to the point I could no longer see the floor.

I suppose he was stunned. There was a jovial jaunt about him for the remainder of the afternoon. He dropped me off with the women from my critique group with a plethora of threats and warnings, but he was different enough that I felt a little bit of hope stir in my spirit.

The writing conference was an incredible opportunity for me. My first picture book had just been published, I felt... *important*. I was meeting people I had only known from online groups. I watched as people discussed their dreams coming true and how the market was changing in the world of children's literature.

Before most attendees' coffees got cold, the conference turned into one great disaster for me. All the gleaming faces, talented brains, and wonderful humans were running elated circles around me while I... was stuck to my phone. My husband didn't want me to miss a single message he'd sent. He was reading the first book in the series. I was being informed of his expectations, but most importantly, all the ways I was already not living up to them.

Instead of listening to the prospective agents and editors I was hoping to submit my work to, I was reading text messages that told me I was only ever to refer to him as *Sir*. When I asked what he meant, he called me. I raced out of the conference hall and into a breakout session room, but organizers were setting up chairs. I didn't answer in time, so I knew I was in trouble. I called him back as soon as I got to somewhere quiet, but it was too late.

"You will answer when I call; I don't give a fuck what you're doing. You are mine, and I allowed you to go to this. I come first. Do you understand?"

"Yes."

"Yes, WHAT?"

"What do you mean?"

"Oh, this is going to be fun. *You* wanted this life, right? I told you. You will refer to me as *Sir*. So, it's 'Yes, SIR.'"

"Okay... I'm sorry—"

"Sorry, WHAT? Ohhhh, you're in for it now. When you get home, you'll be shown why you won't forget to call me 'Sir.'"

What had I done?

I could taste my mascara-laden tears as I tried to hold it all in. I was in public, for heaven's sake. I couldn't get to my makeup bag to do a touch-up. What had I done? Did I just make my life worse? *What had I done??*

"Yes... *Sir*."

"That's better. Go back to your conference. Don't waste my money."

My friends, this is where my life took a turn. The days, weeks, and months that followed were ones of walking on eggshells like nearly no one can understand. *I* didn't understand. I was getting more attention from him, which was all I had ever wanted from anyone. He would send me flirty text messages, bring home bottles of wine, take me places—the works! I had to be on my best behavior, of course, but it felt incredible to be seen again. And as long as I didn't mess up or make him angry, I could live this new life.

However, as time went on, our relationship quickly became nothing more than sex. It revolved around sex in such a negative manner that I couldn't make a simple dinner without dreading the hours that would follow it. Those flirty messages? They became promises or threats. The bottles of wine turned into harder liquor and were mainly consumed by him. All the places we went to together became battles I was incapable of winning because I wasn't allowed to speak to other people (especially men).

I was no longer allowed to look my husband in the eyes. My head had to be bowed when I spoke to him.

I was no longer allowed to touch my husband—not on the shoulder, not in a hug, nor to hold his hand—without asking permission first.

The books I had read were not like this. The BDSM, D/s lifestyle is not like this, as rules must be accepted and understood by both parties.

My youngest child—a wee toddler at the time—asked me, "Mommy, you k?" far too often.

Is this marriage? Is this really how it's supposed to be?

I was trapped. And I'd done it to myself.

5

"We've got to live, no matter how many skies have fallen."

— D. H. LAWRENCE

NARCISSISTIC ABUSERS THRIVE ON THEIR VICTIM'S DISORIENTATION. The constant questioning and doubt the victim suffers feeds the abuser's incessant and unrelenting hunger. I can attest that the daily rounds I went with myself, wondering if I was losing my mind, went on so long that I eventually believed I was going insane.

Can you take a second and picture that for a moment? As a grown adult, you walk around with your children, go to church, wash the dishes... just absolutely aimless, fearing that you had an early onset of dementia or severe mental illness. You cannot comprehend how the world works any longer because you don't believe a single word *anyone* says to you, save for your abuser. Your abuser knows all, don't they?

That was my reality by the end of 2012. The downhill speed at which I was being hurled from who I used to be into this lifeless shell of a human was unmatched.

Our oldest child had been diagnosed with epilepsy, which threw us for a loop we were unprepared for. They were failing medication after medication—seizing worse on each one we gave them. Despite multiple tests and hospital stays, we weren't getting the answers we needed to help our little one.

As if that wasn't enough, my mother had gone missing, was found after a few weeks of searching, only to briefly move in with us just as Christmas (and my husband's drinking habits) reared its jolly head. I hadn't seen nor spoken to my mother in over three years—we had a tumultuous relationship at best. She was disabled, not working, and heavily addicted to pain medication. She'd been that way for years, which caused trauma and pain like no other. I was forced to become the mother of my household when I was about 12 years old—but that's another book I have yet to write.

I was under much pressure from my mother's side of the family to take care of her, despite my oldest child's seizure activity, our insane lifestyle, and the fact that she needed a convalescent-type living center (but was only 51 years old). She qualified for no government housing. She was too young for a retirement home. My husband drank excessively and punished me nightly for keeping her in our home. At one point, I found her passed out in our youngest child's room with a plethora of pills strewn across the carpet. Our youngest, only three years old, was holding a few pills in their hand, and my husband (rightfully, I admit) lost his mind.

He screamed at my mother, dragged me by my hair to our room, and told me she needed to get out. He said I had to call my mother's sister and tell her that my mother had to go somewhere else, or he'd call the police.

I couldn't tell anyone that my husband had a drinking problem and that I was afraid for my life. I certainly did not want my mother's family to think I was putting her in danger.

So, I did what I could to make up a story about her being unable to stay with us for Christmas, and that if I could, I would find her a place to live while she visited them for the holiday season. My aunt was hesitant but didn't know me well enough to notice my behavior change.

I wish she had known how many times I locked myself in my bathroom to scream and cry over the issue. I put on an angry front, taking a lot of my pain and anger out on my mother. In truth, she deserved unending backlash from years of neglect, lies, and abuse. But that wasn't the time or the right way to do it.

I put her on the plane for her visit a week or so prior to Christmas, and my husband "rewarded" me with an orgasm.

Several acts that caused severe trauma led to my brain perhaps permanently blocking out how 2013 began: While she was away, my mother decided to move in with my aunt and uncle, about 500 miles away; my oldest child was seizing upwards of 10 times a day—with no medications helping and the word "surgery" being thrown around a little *too* often; my youngest baby was growing before my eyes without me being functional enough to see it; and my husband—whom I officially and not so affectionately called my *monster* in my head— couldn't end his nights without getting drunk, tying me up, and trying a new concoction of BDSM maneuvers that would please him immensely, and leave me in pain.

My body was so tired. My hair was falling out, and my doctor was growing concerned. She told me I should see a therapist and think about getting more rest. *Ha... Who knew this doctor was a comedian?* I laughed myself right out of her office. Pushing through each day was all I was able to do. People in my life who only knew the bare minimum of what was happening in my world would always ask me, "How do you do it?" I'd smile, shrug my shoulders, and offer them the same line time after time: *What choice do I have?*

I had to push through. I'd made this mess; I had to see my way out of it.

When I took my mother to the airport so she could fly to her new home, something told me to take a couple of pictures with her. She wasn't quite sober but was clear-minded enough to stand steady. I asked my five-year-old to take my camera and try their best to take a picture of Grammie and me. It was a bit shaky, but they were proud of themselves. Both kids took a picture with the woman they'd only just gotten to know and were squealing with delight when she made a silly toot-like noise to get them to smile for the camera.

She was solemn and slow to move. I couldn't help but feel like I was betraying her, like I was surrendering a dog to the animal shelter—a dog I'd adventured with my whole life, whose only sin was that they were getting too old for me to take care of. She meant the world to me; she was my mother, for goodness' sake. The look in her eyes was unbearable. She was deeply wounded but clearly felt she deserved it. She probably thought she'd done it to herself.

Heh... like mother, like daughter.

What was I doing—was I abusing *her* now? Was I in a position of power and enjoying watching her suffer? Certainly not. But that knowing in her spirit spread across her forehead and weighed heavily across her shoulders. I couldn't take it. I felt like the scum of the earth.

I hugged her so tightly. In between inconsolable sobs, I told her I loved her and that I was sorry. I told her to forget moving so far away and to stay with me, that I was in trouble in my marriage, and was terrified he was going to kill me. I begged her —asking that we run away together, saving the kids and ourselves. We could go anywhere! We could change our numbers, find simple jobs, homeschool the kids, and leave the country when we'd saved enough money. We'd make it work. We were survivors. We'd find a way!

"This way through security, Ma'am."

I snapped back into reality, and my mother was walking away. *Of course,* I hadn't said what I wanted to. *Of course,* I let her go without much more than a tear-filled goodbye.

"Bye, Bethie. I love you."

"I love you, too, Momma."

I should have stopped her. I should have forgiven her then and there and borne her burden on my shoulders just a little longer. At that point, I'd done it for over 20 years; what was a little longer?

She passed through security and turned to look back at me, flashing that smile I'd looked for from my existence. As numb as I was, I managed to wave back, hoping she could see the brokenness and fear in my eyes. She couldn't have believed my mask. She knew I was lying about how good my life was, didn't she? She was coming back for me and would make things better like she did when I was a babe... right?

She slipped away from my view into the long hallways of the airport.

That was the last time I saw my momma.

Six months later, she passed away suddenly—her body giving in to the punishment she'd rendered to herself after years of abuse, blame, guilt, and shame.

I was stuck in my cage, unable to save her. Unable to be with her, hold her, whisper in her ear how she was the best mom despite all the chaos. I couldn't touch her. I couldn't even identify her body or ask for a private moment from the coroner to lie next to her. I wasn't allowed to leave my house. I was required to stay because we had children to care for, and I had mouthed off at the wrong time while a certain someone was driving to Colorado for yet another assignment.

I never got to say goodbye.

My disorientation grew.

My monster prevailed.

I wanted to be buried with her. I screamed until I spit blood, unsure why God was so cruel. Surely, He'd let me go with her. He'd take me home. I wanted nothing more of the façade that was my life.

"Mommy? Can we Facetime Grammie in Heaven?"

My kids. My angels. My gifts. I had my children. If I didn't live for them, who would? I couldn't—there was no way I could allow them to grow up without a mother. I had basically done that myself, and look where it had gotten me. No, it wasn't time for me to join her. But, dear heavens, did I want to the moment my monster walked in the door three days after my cousin called me with the news.

I needed love. I needed consoling, care, and loads of compassion. I needed all the grace one could muster in order to have outbursts of hysterical tears, anger, and confusion. I needed space to understand my feelings. I needed to be *allowed* to have feelings.

Those were not given to me.

I was allowed to be thankful that my husband came home from his assignment, but I had to understand that life still goes on, and we still had bills to pay.

Four days after my mother's passing, I had to whisk our oldest off to the hospital, where they would stay for over a week. Major tests needed to be done, including a Positron Emission Tomography scan (PET scan) and a Magnetoencephalography (MEG scan) to determine the areas of their brain where their seizures stemmed from. My mother's body was still in the morgue, and I already had to address the other source of severe hurt and worry in my life. I remember the nurses (who had become family to us at that point) noticing my unusual fatigue.

"Are you okay? Is this stay hitting harder because we're looking at surgery now?" She was my dearest friend in that hospital, and I didn't even know her name. Lost in my sweltering headache, heartache, and fear of the unknown, I looked at her and gasped for air. She caught me as I collapsed. She held me on the floor as I cried. She stayed with me for an hour, just listening to me sob. The only words I could get out were, "I'm so sorry," and, "It's just too much." Between handing me tissues and stroking my hair, she told me I wasn't allowed to be sorry.

Funny, my momma always said that.

The moment I got home with our child after all the tests had been taken and all the "We'll call you when we find the answer" lines had been said, I said goodbye to my monster, who was off on another assignment. I was grateful, in a way, because, at the very least, I could concentrate on putting together a memorial for my mother. Sadly, I had to do so without the help of her family as her sister, my aunt, was speaking to me less and less as the days went on. When we did speak, the uncomfortable, hostile tones were more than I could bear. She was angry with me, but why? Because I had asked for help with my mother —*her* sister? Did that force her in some way to face the truths that I had been speaking for over a decade about my mom? Didn't she understand I lived in an ever-growing abusive situation with two children under six, one seizing 15 to 50 times a day?

It didn't matter. *She* lost *her* sister, and I was more than likely the reason. She must have seen me as a demon—an ungrateful child who tossed my mother to the wind, just as my father had done. If she only knew... maybe things would have been different.

Honestly, it felt like she'd died too, along with my cousins I was so close to. They were angry at me for something they didn't understand. I couldn't blame them; my ability to fend for myself was nonexistent, and thinking I was worth anything other than the lies my monster said about me was useless.

I was blessed by the church my family attended when I was a child, as they offered to have my mother's memorial in one of their buildings. We quickly put it all together, letting everyone know via social media about the day. I asked those who planned to come to bring a dish, making it a potluck funeral because I couldn't afford to have it catered. It felt so thrown together, so minuscule, versus the memorial my mother deserved. That added more guilt.

So, I decided to make a video—an homage to who my mother was. I chose a song that meant everything to me, that said all I couldn't say. I placed each photo delicately to emphasize the lyrics perfectly. It was my heart, in song, through pictures... something I focused all my efforts on so that I could grieve properly. It was the only escape I'd had between the news of her death, staying in the hospital for a week with my child just four days later, and my monster forcing me to have sex with him without complaining (not to mention getting tied up and whipped until my skin cracked because of my "bad attitude").

I ended the montage with perhaps my favorite picture of her that I took the day I'd found her again—the day she said she was saved, the day I'd washed her hair and blown it dry. "Wow, I look so beautiful, Sissy!" she'd said when I showed her the photo. It was definitely a gut-wrenching ending to the video because, well, it showed my mom's degression. But that was not the intention. I loved that picture—and love it still. I actually take that picture with me everywhere I go, still to this day.

For some reason, my aunt wanted to see the video I'd made. My intuition told me she was looking for something—wanting to prove that I was out to hurt my mother, somehow, some way. Boy, was I ever right. The email I received, the phone call I got... my goodness. I was a terrible daughter. She couldn't understand why I would put that last picture in and demanded I remove it. She even went as far as to tell me she would ask my mother's best friend on the day of the memorial (because, of course, my aunt wouldn't be there) if I'd removed it. I was gutted. This was *my* gift. This was the only way I could grieve, and even *that* was wrong and was taken from me.

Out of fear, I removed the picture. I removed a couple of others, too, just in case my aunt disapproved.

It wasn't my gift any longer. It wasn't my chance to grieve.

The day came and went, and my mother was celebrated beautifully. The place was packed; so many people came to share stories of how my mother had saved their lives... literally. Each story ended with an apology, though—an apology to my mother for not being there for her, an apology to my brother and me for not believing us when we said she was in trouble.

Each and every story.

I felt a touch of vindication, but it wasn't enough to help close this horrific chapter in my life. If anything, this was the launching pad of chaos—as everything from then on would lead me to write this book.

QUICK WARNING!

IF YOU ARE NOT IN A PLACE MENTALLY OR EMOTIONALLY TO HANDLE DESCRIPTIONS OF PHYSICAL ABUSE, NOW IS THE TIME TO TAKE A BREAK. PUT THIS BOOK DOWN, GO SPEND TIME WITH LOVED ONES OR EVEN WITH ANIMALS.

It's self-care time.

PLEASE, <u>PLEASE</u> do not read on until you are ready.

YOU ARE LOVED. YOU ARE NEEDED. YOU ARE IMPORTANT.

6

"Now she can handle the pain. It is the little voice in her head that reminds her of how long she's handled it that haunts her."

— *JMSTORM*

2013... A YEAR THAT WILL FOREVER BE MARKED IN HISTORY AS A year that changed me and my stance on humanity as a whole. There were no months, no specific sunsets to mark the days; 2013 just *was*. When I concentrate, I can recall the date my mother died, the dates of my oldest child's surgeries, and the date of my monster's first arrest. I won't lie, though; remembering those things takes a lot of focus—which is disconcerting to me because remembering dates has always been a random superpower I've delighted in having. I don't remember what happened on my children's birthdays, my birthday, or what we did for Thanksgiving or Christmas that year. I barely recall a big family reunion trip we took with my father's side of the family, celebrating his stepmother's 70th birthday.

2013 was a blur.

A date that I remember from birth was July 25 because it was the day my parents married. In 2013, they would have celebrated 32 years. Instead, my mother was dead, my father was cavorting with a woman I detested, and I officially became a victim of provable domestic violence.

Now, I will warn you that what follows is graphic. Please understand that I am writing this as a source of understanding, help, and solidarity. If your story is similar, you are not alone. If you are in the throes of abuse right this minute, YOU ARE NOT ALONE. Please refer to the beginning and end of this book for resources to help you. Do not allow one more minute of your life to be stolen because of fear. You CAN survive; you WILL survive.

If you are reading this and have never been in a position of abuse, this is the moment where I ask that you pause. Close your eyes. Thank God, or whomever you believe in, and ask that others around the world be as fortunate as you. Ask for peace in the hearts of the hurting. Ask for safety, strength, and clear, LOUD voices to set them free from their bonds as victims. They matter, and so do their stories.

Perhaps you can volunteer at a shelter where women and their children flock, hiding in fear they cannot describe. Maybe you can call a friend you've always been concerned for but never had the guts to step in and say something. Trust me, you have friends in my position. They're in your schools, your neighborhoods, and most especially, in your churches. I would have done just about anything to have had just ONE friend speak up and help me. Think about it... you could be the difference in someone's life—or their emotional, mental, or even physical death.

I DON'T REMEMBER why he was home from work that day. He usually had Mondays and Tuesdays off, but it was in the middle of the summer. He'd taken time off for my mother's memorial the Saturday before; perhaps he took that Thursday off because he was forced to. There wasn't much to the day—the usual errands to run, kids fighting their naps, and waiting on phone calls from the hospital for our oldest. I was focused on getting dinner done and letting the children play outside in the sprinklers. I ran to the restroom while my husband's phone rang. As I passed by him, I crossed my fingers, hoping he was getting called for another assignment. When I returned to the kitchen, my husband's demeanor was different. He was... *dark*.

"That was the hospital. They gave us the first round of surgery dates. August 26, they're doing the Burr Hole procedure. They're going to drill holes into our child's skull. August 26. A month from tomorrow."

Horrified, I asked how he knew this. It turned out they called him—something the hospital had *never* done—and not me. He announced that he needed to go to the store and asked the children to go with him. He made a small dig at me, saying I could cry alone that way, but dinner needed to be done when he got back.

I was lost. I was alone. I couldn't grasp what was happening, what would happen. I did what I'd always done, and I went numb. I stayed positive because, at the very least, we weren't waiting around for that call any longer. I called the head nurse at the epilepsy center and got better details about what needed to be done. I had her write in our file notes that my husband was *never* to be contacted unless it was an emergency. She apologized for the mix-up and said she'd see me soon.

I finished dinner and waited for them to return. I posted to Facebook about the update and felt a little relief that the community who loved our child so much was raining down notes of love, prayers, and positivity. I thought that maybe, just maybe, we could do this.

He walked in the door with only a couple of bags. The kids sat at our table as he unloaded his purchases onto the counter. Two six-packs of a dark IPA, a bottle of rum, a Long Island Iced Tea mix, and two bottles of wine.

I was annoyed because I wanted to talk about the phone call. But he popped his first beer, chugged it down, slammed it on the counter, and opened another. .

We ate dinner. We pretended like nothing had happened. I was checking my phone constantly, looking at the comments on Facebook—my hope, my tribe, my life-giving community of support. He caught me with my phone a couple of times. That made him angry. He shouted at me, but I was in such a state I actually shouted back (a big, *big* no-no). He was pretty tipsy at that point, so he didn't do more than raise his hand at me and threaten me "with a good time."

I asked him to put the alcohol down, telling him we needed to talk about what was going on. He laughed dismissively and told me to go to hell. I don't know what came over me—it was like 6,000 ancestors of mine billowed their strength in my direction because I reached for the can in his hand. I held onto it and asked him, again, to put it down. He shoved me. Not once, but twice. I flew across the kitchen and hit my head on our pantry's doorknob. Everything went black.

I came to, hazily, with him standing over me, yelling that I was faking it. My four-year-old was screaming, "Mommyyy!" My husband left my view, and I could hear him carrying our children to their rooms. He shouted for them to stay there, saying Mommy was in trouble and needed punishment.

Imagine being four and six years old. Imagine the fear that must have struck in them. A lump still swells in my throat at the thought.

I don't remember much until I was hurled over his shoulder and slammed onto our bed. I was able to speak at that point, and I shouted that I wasn't faking it, that he'd hurt me.

"Well, call 911 then! Oh, you're being abused? You poor little girl! You KNOW you're lying, and they'll know it too. You shouldn't have grabbed my beer out of my hand! Your head is fine. Don't lie. Let the cops show up! Hmm, who will they believe? A lying piece of shit woman, or me... a fellow cop who they've probably worked with? My rig is out front! They won't even stop for you."

He threw my phone at my face, told me not to move, and walked out of our room. Things were still hazy for me, so I'm not sure how much time went by. I heard him in the kitchen mixing a drink. He turned the TV up so loud; I just knew the kids must have been terrified and unable to sleep. I went out to kiss them goodnight and assure them everything would be okay, but I had to be careful. I couldn't let my monster see me. They hugged me and asked me to sing to them like always.

"Not tonight, guys. I need you to go to sleep."

"Mommy, the sun is still way up high..."

"I know it is, I know. The sun is just playing tricks on us. I need you to go to sleep, okay?"

"But we didn't brush our teeth!"

"Surprise! Tonight, you don't have to—and you can stay in one bed together. I—"

I heard a cup being set down on our slate coffee table in the living room. I was a goner. I just couldn't let the kids see. As calmly as I could, I tucked them both into the youngest's bed and kissed their foreheads, begging God not to let a tear fall from my welled-up eyes.

I raced back to our bedroom. My husband was grabbing a beer from the refrigerator; he didn't see me.

I jumped back onto our bed just as he walked in.

"Are you done with your lies now?"

"I wasn't lying, Sir. You really—"

SLAM.

My head hit the bed. He didn't hit me but pushed me down so hard that I hit our mattress with a slap. His hand was on the back of my neck with what felt like his entire body weight.

"Oh, so a little girl like you is going to lie about how much her bitch ass lies? It's my lucky day!"

"Please don't, you already hurt my head. Please, Sir. Just stop!"

"I did nothing. You fell on your own! What a stereotype this is, too, right? You gonna call the cops? CALL THEM!"

"No, Sir, I am not going to call the cops—please let me go."

His hand came off my neck, but he soon had both my arms behind me. He was laughing like a madman.

"I want to go to sleep. I don't need to hear any more of your whining. You aren't to leave our bed, not for any reason!"

He fell asleep almost immediately. I waited, holding as still as possible. An hour went by. He was snoring so loudly that I believed I was safe. I snuck out to grab the children and run, but by the time I got to their door, I heard him yelling.

"You're FUCKING kidding me, right? Oh, you're going to pay for this."

I locked our youngest's bedroom door and thanked God we hadn't changed the doorknob on that door yet. I grabbed the youngest and woke the oldest, holding onto them for dear life as I tried to open their window. My husband was pounding at the door. He was yelling and demanding I open it. Then I heard the hammer on the doorknob. I couldn't help but feel like I was in the ending scenes of *The Shining*, where Jack Torrance was going after Wendy with the axe on the bathroom door.

I'd struggled with the screen but managed to get it off. I scooped up my sleepy six-year-old in the hand not occupied by my fast-asleep four-year-old lying on my shoulder. I got one step out into the flowerbed just outside the window when the door-knob hit the carpet, and my husband had me by the elbow. He ushered the oldest back to their room and told them to stay in bed or he would spank them with a belt. I held the youngest so tightly, thanking God—again—that they were still asleep. My husband closed the window and told me to return to our room so we could talk about this.

I knew better. I knew... I just knew better.

The door slammed and locked behind me. The sun had set, and our blackout curtains kept the streetlight out. No shadow was cast; it was pure darkness in our room.

He picked me up and slammed me—WWE style—onto our bed. It was only then that I noticed he had gotten himself completely naked. He stumbled around a bit but slammed my torso back down when I attempted to get up. He grabbed a fistful of my hair at the nape of my neck and forced my face into our mattress.

"I told you not to leave, didn't I? What do we do to little girls who don't listen to their masters?"

Five-alarm fear was rushing through me. He'd been angry with me and punished me several times for "insubordination" in the past, but this time, I wasn't sure he would stop when I began to pass out. I had to find a focal point—something that kept me breathing and conscious. My babies were all I could think of. I saw their faces and knew that if things got bad, I could *not* give up because they needed me.

He let me up, pulling me like a marionette by my hair and throwing me across the bed. He was belligerent and fuming.

"You gonna call the cops now? Here! CALL THEM! See what happens! I'm untouchable, and you're a LIAR!" He threw the phone, which hit me directly in the mouth. Electricity jolted through my veins; I wanted to scream, grab the phone, and run.

I reached for the phone, but he jumped on top of me, pinning my shoulders down with his knees. The pain was excruciating. He stood at nearly six feet tall and weighed over 200 pounds. I, on the other hand, never made it past five feet tall, and at the time was a whopping 122 pounds. He, in all his nakedness, dug his knees into my shoulders and grabbed my cell phone. Laughing like a lunatic in a horror movie, he typed in 9-1-1 but didn't hit the call button. Instead, he told me that all I had to do was reach up and hit the button myself.

"Go ahead, CALL THEM, princess! See if they'll save you!"

Of course, I couldn't lift my arms because doing so would mean I'd more than likely dislocate my shoulders. He knew that. He continued to chuckle while I struggled and begged him to let me go. He thought he was quite the comedian. Though my pain was becoming unbearable, I focused on not making a sound above a whisper because my oldest wasn't the best sleeper.

That was the toughest part: combatting a drunken monster while protecting my children's innocence.

He grabbed my wrists and rolled off my shoulders in one swift move, twisting my body so I was lying face down once again. In an instant, my hands were behind my back in his left hand, and his right forearm was against my throat, pulling me closer to his chest. His pores reeked of the copious alcohol he'd consumed, now sweating onto his skin. He flexed his bicep and restricted my airway. Managing to get my hands loose, I quickly elbowed him in the stomach and tried to push his arm up and off me like my 9th grade PE teacher taught me to do in our mini self-defense class she'd offered us girls. It worked, but only for a moment.

If anything, I'd only infuriated him more.

He grabbed me and put me in a half-nelson, slamming my face back onto the bed again. This time, I felt something cold against my skin—my phone! I could see the screen was lit up, but I wasn't close enough or able to touch it. At this point—still laughing, of course—he rolled into me, causing my face and mouth to be consumed by our comforter. My ability to breathe was dwindling. I was screaming. I couldn't think of what else to do. I was terrified that I was going to die, but even more terrified that my children would come looking to find out why Mommy sounded hurt. He kept chanting about how I should have listened to my master and how I needed to learn my lesson.

I briefly glimpsed my still-lit phone as he pulled me up and slammed me back down again. It looked as if... it was! It was on a call. It had dialed. Could it mean what I thought?

The doorbell rang.

He let go and cackled like a cartoon witch flying across the night sky.

"Are you serious? Did you really? How did you manage *that*, baby?"

He walked out of our room. I grabbed my phone and heard the front door open.

"Sir, can you clothe yourself, please?"

"Nah, tell me why you're here, brother. I'll get dressed when I'm ready."

"Sir, find some clothes, and we can talk outside. Is there a woman in this home?"

"If you can call her that, yeah."

I found my footing and went to the front door. I was shaking... or was the ground moving? Either way, my balance wasn't centered. I walked against the wall until I saw the officers standing in my doorway.

"Ma'am? Are you okay? We got two open-ended calls to our emergency line. What happened tonight?"

I told the officer everything. I did what I could to not water down the details, explaining that my husband was clearly upset over the phone call he'd received about our child. I heard myself become the stereotype: *Please don't take him to jail; he will lose his job, and then we'll lose our insurance. We need that to save our child.*

CLICK, CLICK.

That all-too-familiar sound of handcuffs clasping together and tightening around wrists. But this time, they weren't *my* wrists.

After my monster was escorted into the back of one of three cruisers lining my street—in the dark, of course, to save a fellow officer's embarrassment—my interview grew more in-depth. An officer asked to see our children... *our children! How could I have forgotten about our children??* I ran inside to find both nose-to-glass against the window in our youngest child's room. It was the only window that faced the street.

They saw everything.

I burst into tears and grabbed them, pulling them into my arms like I'd lost them years ago, only to find them again in that moment.

"Why are the police officers here, Mommy? Did they put handcuffs on Daddy? Why did they do that? Is Daddy a dirtbag now, Mommy?"

My shattered heart splintered and tore with every gut-wrenching question pouring from their mouths. I couldn't fathom how to answer them then, so I held their hands, assuring them everything would be okay. That "Daddy made a mistake, but we're going to fix it."

The officers looked over the kids and half-heartedly dismissed them by explaining that he needed to speak with their mommy for a little bit more. I turned on the television and sat them on the couch with their little cups of milk.

Our lives are never going to be the same. Please, God, how are we going to do this?

The officer took pictures of the red marks on my arms and neck while another questioned me about the number of firearms in the house. I had no clue, and if I was completely honest, I hated the things, so it never occurred to me to care. Per protocol, they were required to remove them from our property after arresting an officer of the law. Neither my husband nor I were allowed to have them back until after court proceedings concluded. I was mortified that an officer—a complete stranger —had to go through my messy house, with my devastatingly disgusting walk-in closet that I had not had the chance to clean earlier in the day as I was supposed to (something my "master" claimed I was going to be punished for). This meant that the officer was walking over clothes, *my* clothes—my underwear, for God's sake—in order to get ahold of all the guns and ammunition.

When they had gotten all the information they needed from me, they left me with nothing more than a standard apology and suggestion that I go "get help" if I needed it. I was standing in the front yard of our home, in our cookie-cutter neighborhood, without a hope or prayer in the world. I was breathless, sore, scared out of my mind, and unbelievably unprepared for what was to come.

"Hey, neighbor... You okay?"

Heaven help me.

Our next-door neighbors were standing outside their front door. The husband was a sheriff's deputy, and she was the stay-at-home mom who I couldn't connect with no matter how hard we tried. I burst into tears and told them everything. He walked briskly down the street just as the last officer got into his patrol rig and quizzed him about the situation. After all, *men know more.*

He returned after a few minutes, shaking his head. Thankfully, he gave me a lot of information about what I needed to do next. His helpful advice was to find somewhere else to stay. Didn't he know? I had nowhere else to stay. I didn't have friends

I was allowed to be close to—not in that way. I didn't have family stable enough for me to trust. I was stuck, just like my husband wanted me to be.

At long last, I walked inside, closing the door behind me. My babies were lying on the couch, far past their bedtime, and much too sleepy. I tucked them into my bed, assuring them (assuring myself?) that we were going to be fine. I prayed over their sweet, furrowed brows and sang them to sleep.

Life will be different in the morning.

7

"He wasn't capable of loving you the way you loved, it's not your fault."

— *E. S.*

MY PHONE RANG ALL NIGHT.

"Hello. This is the county jail calling with a collect call from *'Bethany, you better ANSWER ME!'*. Do you wish to accept these charges?"

"Hello. This is the county jail calling with a collect call from *'FUCK YOU FOR DOING THIS TO ME!'* Do you wish to accept these charges?"

"Hello. This is the county jail calling with a collect call from *'Your husband, maybe.'* Do you wish to accept these charges?"

. . .

I COULD GO into detail about each conversation. I could explain that he was terrifying and sounded like he was out for blood because maybe he was. I could discuss how he said we were done, that he never should have married me, that our life was over. But I don't believe the finite details matter all that much. The truth is, I could have ended everything there; I could have left him in jail, pursued the charges stacked against him, and filed for divorce. My children and I might have been able to find safety and security in the few church friends we had and perhaps could have started over.

But that's not what happened.

Since then, long-time friends have personally scolded me for *not* deciding to leave him that night.

And honestly, I understand.

The one thing society claims to know about people in abusive situations, especially women, is that leaving one's abuser is the easiest thing to do. Much like taking a simple breath of air into your lungs, walking away from someone who doesn't treat you right should damn near be second nature because everyone knows how they deserve to be treated. Society consistently alludes that a woman who leaves her abuser is not only believed but also absolutely *welcomed* in each environment she reaches out to. Take a second and think about how many times even you have said, "Why didn't she just leave?" or "I would have helped her if only I'd known," or, "Why didn't she just say something?" or, and perhaps worst of all, "I don't understand how women like that can be so stupid. They should just get up and walk away. It's not hard."

That last sentence was said *to* me by a coworker just last week; granted, they were not talking about me, but still, it wounded me. I've heard things like that said by people who have never been in an abusive situation. Their judgment is based on what they imagine it must be like or how they might react if it were happening to them. They've seen movies or television programs that have depicted such scenarios, so their understanding is easy to come by.

Still, statements like that lead to the most intrusive thoughts for the victims:

How could I have been so stupid? I should have gotten up and walked away that night. It's not hard, after all, right?

It's the words and harsh judgments from others that continuously haunt me. So, instead of going into the details of the day after his arrest, I'm now going to answer the one question that every human I personally know has wanted to ask me since learning about my story, and perhaps get ahead of it and answer the same question that the people I have yet to meet will want to ask me, too...

Bethany, Why Didn't You Leave?

I have asked myself that question at least 2,000 times a day, each day, from the moment I brought him home from jail on July 26, 2013.

I only have one simple answer: My oldest child needed brain surgery to survive.

Without surgery, my eldest's seizures might have gotten to the point where I would have been shopping for a tiny-sized casket instead of back-to-school clothes. Without surgery, my eldest would never have become a triathlete in their first year of high school or won awards no other freshman has received on record in their school's JROTC program. Without surgery, my child would have suffered, plagued with a lifetime of debilitating anguish, and that's if they lived at all.

You see, the day I became a mother, I made a promise—no, I

made it my PERSONAL MISSION—to always take my children's pain on as my own so that they would never have to hurt. Obviously, that's a difficult and not always possible charge a mommy can proclaim for her babies. But I swore to myself and each of my children in the wee hours of those early sleepless nights that I would do all within my power to keep them from harm.

So...

That's what I did.

I posted bail. I walked into that dark, concrete anti-palace with my four- and six-year-old children. With fresh concealer on the bruises on my arms and neck, I requested my monster by name. They handed me a plastic bag with his personal belongings—most noticeably his wedding ring, which he promptly threw at my face as soon as we pushed through the double doors of the jail's exit.

In the following weeks, I stood by his side as he begged to keep his job so that we could keep his health insurance for our child's sake. I went to his mandatory therapy sessions and told a lot of lies to the therapist to make him look saner than he was so that the therapist would give a stellar report to the judge. I called his captain and begged her for her understanding. I wrote to the judge and called the D.A., lying my ass off just so he'd stay out of the prison cell I knew he deserved to rot in.

I had the lie for everyone we knew about why he was home and not off on assignments all over the country, claiming he was a "good father" and was taking a leave of absence from work. "He's wanting to be home while our baby goes through all the surgeries," I'd fib. I endured harassment from my in-laws, who were furious at me for not being "woman enough" to handle a little beating. I sat through countless stories of how "Grandpa put a gun to my temple when we were first married, and *I* didn't call the cops!" and, "He throws shit at me, and I slap him around all the time, and we've been married over 30 years! Get over it!"

and of course, the unrelenting conversations like, "You finally got what was coming to you, and the first thing you did was call the cops? What a bitch! We knew you were no good!"

I'd close my eyes tightly, gritting my teeth and holding my breath.

My child needed surgery.

My child needed surgery.

My child needed surgery.

The justification for me to stay in my marriage seemed as obvious as the need for oxygen. It wasn't that I was stupid or incapable of standing on my own two feet (though my monster had led me to believe otherwise); it was the sheer fact that my little one needed the best care our healthcare system could buy. Unfortunately, in the country in which we live, doctors and surgeons of that quality require an obscene amount of money... *and* the kind of insurance my monster had. There wasn't another choice I could make.

There isn't another choice I'd make again.

AFTER SEVERAL WEEKS OF THERAPY, weekly Celebrate Recovery meetings, and endless fights that lasted well into the wee morning hours, the eggshells I was accustomed to walking on felt a little less sharp. He'd stopped drinking and learned a different vocabulary for relaying self-expression (mostly his anger). We focused on the challenges ahead that would either make or break our family—the first set of surgeries that were scheduled for late August, the impending court date that would determine if he kept his job as a Federal LEO, and the second set of surgeries that would either free our child from their multiple seizures a day or do nothing but add damage and create a completely different way of life for all of us. We had nothing but hope and prayer to live from. Was it progress? Had I made the right choice after all? Had God saved my marriage, and I was being rewarded for my endless faith and servant's heart?

There were moments when I believed we would be okay... many moments, actually. I found myself smiling when he would hug me and feeling pure joy when I watched him play with our children. There were even a few nights that I went to bed thanking God for His mercy and for helping our marriage survive.

Did that mean the abuse had stopped? Had he understood the error of his ways and decided to turn his life around?

There were too many questions that I did not have time to process. But the tension in my shoulders had shifted, so perhaps my budding sense of hope and security was natural.

Soon, it was time for our epilepsy warrior to face their first of four surgeries. This one was considered "simple" and "exploratory." I know, those are just the two most beautiful words every mother wants to hear when discussing their six-year-old's brain, right?

Formally, the surgery is known as an "Intracranial Study," where epileptologists/neurologists use strip electrodes to record cortical electrocorticography (ECOG) and determine if a patient is a good candidate for resective epilepsy surgery. Informally, it is not-so-forgivingly called a "Burr-Hole Procedure," and it is precisely how it sounds: the patient is put under anesthesia, and the surgeon drills two to four holes into the patient's skull. Then, the surgeon slides electrode strips into the holes, laying them onto the brain itself. Those electrodes monitor all seizure activity to determine if the seizures are focal (specified to one area of the brain) or general (stemming from no particular or singular location).

As a family, we stuck together and did what we could to hype our child up and get them the love they deserved during an incredibly scary time. There were even moments where my monster would hold our child and cry. I really believed that in his heart, he loved his kids and wanted them to not only survive but thrive as well. I saw my monster pray... *a lot*. He transitioned into someone I felt I could sort of depend on, though he wasn't in the throes of the hospital stays or conversations with the doctors. He didn't know each nurse by name like I did, nor could he recognize fellow long-term PICU families. But he was there, a little bit at a time. I was grateful. I was hopeful. And I believed that, at least for that time, my monster's anger and abuse were put on a back burner somewhere; I could focus on our child... and focus I did.

The initial procedure went well. Our baby woke up groggy and nauseous, with their head wrapped tightly in what must have been yards of stark white gauze. Half a dozen electrical wires cascaded out of the bandages, and our sweet kiddo looked helpless. Guilt-fueled rage jolted through me like a live wire. My monster could only stay for about an hour because he had to return to our youngest, who was staying with friends. He held our child and played a few rounds of Angry Birds with them.

I paced.

I spoke with every nurse in the PICU and decorated our child's all-glass room with pictures from classmates and notes from loved ones. See, our kid had quite the social media following, as well as loads of loving supporters from all over the world. Even the kind people at *LucasFilm* had sent their number one fan a major care package after they caught wind of the tweet that showed our little one holding up a sign requesting to meet George Lucas. I made sure our pillows and blankets from home adorned the hospital bed and framed pictures of our family covered tabletop surfaces.

In other words, I went to work. I couldn't stomach just sitting there. I was so deeply devoted to helping our child survive that my rose-tinted glasses must have cracked a bit. I became over-whelmed, wanting my monster to leave. Suddenly, I could only see his fakeness: the doting, loving father who would move heaven and earth for his offspring had to have been a mask. Lest we forget that a mere month prior, he was sitting in a holding cell, wearing one of his federal marijuana eradication unit shirts inside out for fear of the beatdown he might receive if one of the others found out he was a cop. I was ecstatic when he left.

If I could be so bold in admitting anything about myself during those days, I can say that I was running on fumes. I did not drink alcohol, do any drugs, or self-medicate in any way. Hell, I didn't even touch Tylenol. I was afraid that any substance I added to my already hectic life would render me an addict like my mother and my husband. Take a second, though, and realize what I had been through in about 80 days–my mother's passing, planning and executing her memorial service, my monster's physical abuse and arrest, keeping up multiple lies, and straining myself mentally just to keep my marriage in order, running an epilepsy support group for over 100 mommas, helping my youngest child navigate preschool, and finally, my oldest child's brain surgery. I have no clue how I kept pushing.

But push, I did.

8

———

"And then she told herself, 'Stop being so weak. Grow up and get over it.' and she never felt anything again."

— *UNKNOWN*

I WAS NUMB.

Numb to reality and how the world worked. I only understood grueling, nagging pain. From sunup to sundown, I was putting out fires and obliterating the insecurities and fears of those close to me. No one knew what to say in return. I was surrounded by a support system that only knew a portion of my agony. I was the biggest liar, but there was nothing I could do.

The in-between time after the Burr-Hole procedure was done and the major surgery set to alter our ideas of life as we knew it was... well... nothing to highlight. We were at home, thanking God that our oldest-born had survived the early stages of chaos. We genuinely attempted to make life as normal for our children as possible—attending back-to-school functions, interacting in church events, and going on outings such as the zoo and our favorite frozen yogurt place. The memories here are non-existent for me, as I cannot even recall my 28th birthday, which happened around then.

Looking back, I find myself asking—*How long can a person remain in shock?*

The simple fact was we were waiting to find out if my monster would be allowed to keep his job or if he would have to serve time in jail for what he'd done to me. His court date was set for the second week of October—the Monday after my ten-year high school reunion.

THAT night, I do remember.

Holy awkwardness, Batman.

High school reunions, especially the first ones, have a stigma about them that no one can deny. It's been ten years since most classmates have seen each other. The pressure to have achieved some level of superiority in your first decade of adulthood is undoubtedly placed upon all humans—at least American humans. I fell into that trap easily and was surprised that my monster did, too. He was four years my senior and did not attend the same high school I did. Not in a million years did I think he would allow me to go, but he handed me his debit card and encouraged me to get a new dress. A NEW DRESS!

I walked through the mall calmly, though I was ready to spontaneously combust from excitement on the inside. I searched for the most perfect yet least expensive dress I could find. I went into dressing room after dressing room, just for the fun of it. I'd liken the experience to when Pinocchio was granted the wish of his dreams, becoming a *real* boy. My brain and emotions were on overdrive, and I felt like I was *finally* getting ahold of what I assumed was life. I remember smiling at other people, keeping my eyes up when I spoke to the cashiers. I wasn't cowering or worrying about being in trouble. Despite my monster's arrest, I distinctly remember *this* moment as the first one where I realized just how disturbing my life was. I loved being out among people without fear. Who knew that could be such a fantastic feeling?

I found a little black dress that hugged my frame, while being mindful of my monster's rules about modesty. I knew the plunging neckline might be a little risky, but damn, if it didn't make me feel like a million bucks. Upon showing him, I would phrase it: "I bought it with the intention that you can take it off me with ease later this evening."

God, I hated myself and what I'd been reduced to.

At my reunion, I had a lot to show: I'd lost over 20 pounds since graduation, had been married almost nine years, had two beautiful children, was a published author, and owned a house. I wanted the shock-and-awe of it all and nothing more. I didn't honestly care what was happening in anyone else's lives. I was merely thrilled to finally be seen and focused on something other than the war that was my home life.

It was lovely catching up with old classmates, though the ones I wanted to spend time with the most were not there. I could look the part as one of the few who had married someone who hadn't run in our circles. I boasted about our children, lamented about my mother (whom everyone knew because she was a beloved sign language interpreter on our campus), and introduced my Federal LEO monster. I spoke little about my life as an agented author or the dreams I had yet to achieve.

Funny, after all the years of watching *Romy and Michelle's High School Reunion*, my expectations were certainly not met. I made a silent vow to myself that by the time our 20th reunion came around, my life wouldn't be the way it was that night. My children would be 16 and 14 by then. I'd have a life I could be honest about and proud of.

The following day, my monster had his court appearance. I

had already called the District Attorney to let him know I'd lied —and worse, that the police officer lied in his report (my most sincere apologies to that officer, who may have received some trouble of his own on my behalf). I'd helped my monster recite what he needed to say and worked with his lawyer to ensure all stories collaborated correctly.

While he was in court, I stayed home with our children. I talked to my friend Lisa on the phone—my only saving grace, who knew *nothing* of the situation in my household. She and I chatted like it was any other day, exchanging mom stories. She never knew how much normalcy she brought to my life. I always felt like the worst friend for deceiving her. As the hours went on, our oldest seized three different times, I put our youngest down for a nap, and then... I fell to my knees in prayer. With tears in my eyes and fire in my lungs, I prayed something like this:

> *God. HOW DARE YOU. How dare You put me in this place where I have to pray for something I do not want. I want him to go to jail. I want freedom from him and his abuse. I want to run freely with these children and raise them in Your eyes, in the safety of Your umbrella. But no. Instead, I have to pray, ask, and beg that You grant [my monster] favor here. He cannot lose his job. He cannot lose his health insurance. [Our oldest child] needs to have these surgeries so [they] can live the life You meant for [them] to have. PLEASE, even though I'm so tired and so pissed at You, PLEASE save us. PLEASE convince the judge to let [my monster] go. PLEASE.*

When my monster walked in through the door, he scooped up both of our children, crying. "It's over! It's over! I can go back to work! Praise God!"

I rejoiced on the outside.

But one of my last beacons of hope within me was extinguished.

9

"To be a good mother while my heart was breaking was one of the hardest roles I've ever had to play."

— *WORD PORN*

GAME FACE ON. IT WAS SURGERY TIME.

The third of four for our little six-year-old. To say I was a mess wouldn't accurately describe how I felt. I could write an entire book on just the feelings of that brisk October morning, all on its own. The echoes of so many of my friends and followers on social media were racing through my veins:

You're SO strong.

How do you do it? Praying for you!

You've got this, Mama! I couldn't do what you're doing.

You're so brave! You and [your child] are such warriors! You're so strong.

I wanted to slap yet hug all of them. They didn't know. They had no idea. And whose fault was that?

Yeah. Exactly.

I kissed my little treasure goodbye as the doctors and nurses flooded the waiting areas, making sure—double, triple, quadruple sure—I was prepared in case *any* of the first, second, or third stages of these surgeries didn't go expected. I signed forms I wouldn't wish on anyone, let alone a parent of a child who still had most of their baby teeth and cuddled with a blankie every night. When they wheeled our baby away, I collapsed. My legs gave out, and I could no longer walk upright. My monster had kindness in his spirit that day. He helped me up, and we went to a patio somewhere to drink something warm and... wait.

The first surgery was where they placed a grid across our child's brain. They cut out a bone flap, removed it, placed the grid delicately on the area of the brain they believed the seizures were stemming from, turned on the electrodes within it, then lightly placed the bone flap on our child's skull, securing it into place with who-knows-what. That procedure alone took nearly seven hours, kiss goodbye to kiss hello.

My father had taken our youngest for us for a couple of days and would bring them to us sometime after the first surgery. I was exceedingly grateful for that gift because, monster as he was, at least I wasn't completely alone while waiting to find out our child's fate.

I wrote a blog about the ins and outs of hospital life. It kept me grounded, focused, and helped me feel some control. I wasn't sure what else I really *could* do, you know? Other than being there for my child, there was nothing else. I kept pushing.

I smiled for my baby when their eyes were on me and cried myself to sleep in that oh-so-luxurious aquamarine chair that was my bed for over two weeks.

My monster was there, too. He really was. He stayed in the Ronald McDonald house with our other child and got beautifully great at knowing how I like my chai from Starbucks and Peet's Coffee. He would text me occasionally in the later hours of the night to see how we were but let me take charge of the goings on at the hospital. After what happened over the summer, I made it a point never to allow the hospital staff to have much contact with him without my presence. I didn't trust him and didn't want to lose the opportunity to know *exactly* what was happening.

Our precious kiddo took a turn for the worse. Their eyes (mainly their left) and entire face swelled up to the point of being completely unrecognizable. They weren't eating. Their ability to breathe was becoming more and more strained. I wound up screaming for the nurses in the PICU at 1:30 a.m. because my baby's labored breaths were slowing beyond what was comfortable for me. They asked me to leave the room. I refused. They brought in a crash cart, three more doctors, pulled seven vials of blood, gave oxygen, and huddled so close around my baby that I could only see the tiniest glimpse of a finger on their left hand.

With tears cascading from my eyes, I cried out to God once again:

Do NOT do this to my baby. Do NOT do this to me. We've been too good; we've been too faithful. Literally, CAN WE PLEASE HAVE SOME GOOD?? Keep my baby alive. Keep [them] alive and help [them] to live a life that [THEY] deserve and can be proud of! Don't You dare do this! I rebuke this plan—even if it IS YOUR plan! Do not, do not, do not!!

"There we are! Hey, kid. Can you hear us?"

A nurse grabbed my hand and pulled me from my chair just outside our room. Was she talking to me or my little one? I looked over and peeking through a tiny slit of skin that used to be an eye socket, I saw my baby's eye. They hadn't gone into cardiac arrest, but—as it turns out—my child was in near-fatal anaphylactic shock. They were allergic to the antibiotic they were being given. None of us knew. At that point, they'd been on it for over 48 hours. It's a wonder they weren't dead.

Truthfully, I flipped God off. My anger was growing, and the only one strong enough to bear it was the "Almighty" upstairs. I was thankful for the days when my mother let me know it was okay to be angry at God. She said I could be angry, but do not act out on that anger by doing something you can't take back. So, with my middle finger in the air and tears catching on my chin, I hugged my baby and thanked God for sparing their life.

A week went by, and not enough seizure activity presented itself. The neurology team wanted to capture a minimum of five seizures so that the grid inside my child's head could accurately depict where the seizures were coming from. The team went in and forced seizures to happen. The momma bear in me almost caused a scene that would have landed me in prison watching that happen. But my monster held me back. I suppose I owe him for that.

After about ten days, the team decided they'd gotten enough. Now was the time for *the* surgery, where they would resect/remove the part of our child's beautiful brain that was causing them to seize so many times a day. We'd had family visit, which was wonderful but chaotic. The chaos wasn't with their presence but more within my heart as I watched my baby yearn to interact with their cousins the way they always did. We'd had our room filled to the brim with Star Wars regalia and notes from home. Our little one had been showered in infinite amounts of love. But the time had come.

I had put together a little book filled with pictures of the people in our child's life. Under each picture was a name. *Mommy, Daddy, [Sibling], Grandpa, Auntie Lisa.* I was told to do this by his neurologist before we came to the hospital in case our child's hippocampus had to be partially or fully removed. In other words, I was preparing for my child to have forgotten everything they'd learned in their six years of life, including... me.

The goodbye was agony. My monster cried. I held it together because the surgeon allowed me to walk into the operating room with my baby. I held them close as they were placed on the table. I did not, did *not* want to let go. This child from my body, from *my soul,* might not make it back to me.

"Don't worry, Mommy. I'm only a little afraid of surgery. God said He'd be with me. And... we hafta believe God."

Yes, baby... we hafta.

The O.R. doors closed behind me. I felt shattered, incapable of breathing air on my own. My monster grabbed me by the forearm (triggering a different fear altogether) and walked me to the cafeteria. Again, we found ourselves waiting—holding tight to our child's blankie and special puppy. I don't remember speaking for the entirety of the nine-and-a-half-hour surgery.

My father arrived, bless him, with our other rambunctious baby. This child, guys, was a champion the entire time their sibling was in the hospital. Day after day, night after night, this child had their world turned upside down, too. But they never batted an eye. My monster had taken them to the beach one of the days we were there. The cold air the ocean nearby billowed against their skin, and it was there that this child finally cried. My monster took a picture of our four-year-old wonder staring off into the ocean with their hands behind their back. When asked about it, they replied, "I was just thinking about [my sibling]... and how I want the seizures to go away."

I still have that picture hanging in my living room to this day.

The four of us waited in the final waiting area (who knew there were so many waiting room stages?). My monster was restless, saying awful things about how I was too flirtatious with the medical teams/staff and how I didn't need to take advantage just because we were in the situation we were in.

I also took a picture of myself holding onto our eldest's special blanket to put on the blog later—to show my complete and total brokenness. As the mom of the family, there were and are very few pictures taken of me. I was the family photographer all the time. So, I guess I just wanted to remember my hurt, fear, and ferocity. My monster said I was being vain and ridiculous. I couldn't even be afraid for our child in peace. There was always something.

Finally, when the surgeon came in, he had a little camera in his hand. I was violently shaking.

"Guys, I have good news. Hippocampus is... intact."

My baby. My baby would remember me. My baby would remember their sibling, their friends, their dogs. Thank the heavens.

The surgeon asked if we wanted to see the pictures he took of our child's brain during surgery. I am usually one for blood, guts, and gore, but this idea made me feel nauseated. I looked anyway. I saw the "before" and the "after" pictures and couldn't believe how a brain really does look just like all the prop ones at Halloween time.

My sweet little one. Would this be it? Would this be the last of it?

Time was the only thing that could answer those questions. In truth, over the following five months, our baby had a grand total of 13 seizures. The final two were ones that nearly ended their life. But, since then, our warrior hasn't had a single seizure. In fact, as I write this book, they are preparing for their life in the Air Force... a dream they wouldn't have achieved without surgery. A surgery I wouldn't have been able to afford without insurance. And insurance I wouldn't have been able to provide without...

staying with my monster.

Does that make me some sort of martyr or saint? No, no, it does not. Does it justify my excuses for continuing a life that was hurtful and wrong? Absolutely not. Do I recommend you follow in my footsteps if you are in a similar situation? NO. But perhaps you can understand the answer to the question you've been wanting to ask. Perhaps now you can acknowledge that humans who stay in abusive relationships aren't "stupid." Sometimes, we have our reasons.

And sometimes, there's just no way out.

10

"When you are not fed love on a silver spoon you learn to lick it off knives."

— *LAUREN EDEN*

THERE'S A SCENE AT THE END OF *THE LORD OF THE RINGS* TRILOGY where Frodo is mentioning how odd it is to return to society when society has no clue the lengths to which you've gone or the war you've experienced along the way in your travels. Returning home from the hospital and trying to go back to *normal* life was impossible. Friends seemed uneasy around us because what on earth do you say to a family who has lived through an unimaginable hell? How do you talk about the weather, complain about your in-laws, or make jokes about sitcoms on TV with people who almost lost their child?

I get it.

But we felt the sting of un-comfortability. I felt twice as alienated as I'd already felt, and that was no one's fault but my own. I still kept a giant lie within the walls I'd built around my heart, and I could in no way start to talk about it at that point.

My monster went back to work, where he felt judged by everyone (because *they* all knew what he'd done, that he'd gotten away with it, and that somewhere within him, he wasn't good for the uniform). Disdain started to grow after his first summer back on assignments, and our marriage started to teeter in the wrong direction. The sexual punishments returned, and the requirement to call him "Sir" again became the norm.

How do families solve issues like this when they're already married, have kids, and already own a home and a new-used car, you ask?

They move!

Of course, you move. We had to run from all the ghosts surrounding us, preventing us from living life to our fullest. My monster applied to be transferred to an even more secluded area in the deep mountains, several hundred miles north of where we lived. I won't lie; to say I was ecstatic would be an understatement. I was tired of driving by my mother's old apartment, the courthouse where my monster should have been sentenced to jail, and the corners of streets and sides of highways where I'd been kicked out of the car because I'd said something wrong. I no longer wanted to live where I grew up; I was ready for adventure.

My monster moved to the new location first, leaving me to continue homeschooling our two children (a decision made easily by my eldest's awful school, which paid no attention to seizure first aid protocol), sell the house, and pack up our belongings. Where we were headed and where my monster was residing was roughly eight hours away. So, when I say it was all up to me, it was *all* up to me. I was exhausted, depleted of love, life, joy, and any sense of energy. But, as I was used to at the time, I just kept pushing.

Funny, though... that old and oh-so-familiar thought came right back to me:

It shouldn't be this hard.

After many months of back and forth, we sold the house. After one brief visit, I'd already fallen in love with our new little town and was looking forward to the cooler weather and slower lifestyle. I was hoping this was the break that would finally help our family be a family.

Moving day came. We'd had a little gathering a few days before to say goodbye to beloved church friends, close friends, and friends who were more like family. My monster's brother and sister-in-law showed up, shockingly, and made it really difficult for me to leave. I spent time with our nephews and niece, whom we'd barely known but loved so much. It was a beautiful day, but we were ready to go.

When the last boxes were loaded, I put the dogs in the car and our youngest child in their booster seat and drove away without a glance in my rearview mirror. Like I said, I was leaving behind ghosts... so many ghosts. The memories that haunted me everywhere I went in that town were wreaking havoc on my mental health. I had a memory on each corner. And driving away from them all was the most uplifting experience.

I was sad only because I also felt like I was running away—or I had failed. I couldn't live out the "dream" in our first home or perfect the life of a cookie-cutter wife. Then again, I wasn't living *my* dream, so I was at an odd impasse in my brain. I said goodbye to my father and his new girlfriend, whom I'd grown to really like. He actually cried, which made me see that, on some level, he loved me—as hard as that still was for me to believe. I said goodbye to my Lisa, and *that* was hard. She was my go-to, my "ride or die" at a time when I didn't know how to manage a friendship well. Saying goodbye to her and watching her husband help her into the car because of her broken heart was gut-wrenching.

The drive was exhausting and exhilarating at the same time.

My monster and our oldest kiddo were in the moving truck while I drove a packed car filled with immediate needs, the youngest kiddo, and two up-there-in-years dogs. I loved listening to the children cackle together over the walkie-talkies we'd gotten them for the trip. It was beautiful to see their excitement. But a drive like that gives a girl a long time to sit in her thoughts.

The month we moved in 2015 marked almost exactly two years since my mother had passed, since my monster's arrest, and since the journey down the brain surgery tunnel began. Was I really driving to a place where absolutely *no* help would rescue me if I needed it? I mean, I barely had help before, but at the very least, I knew our entire county like the back of my hand. In this new area, I couldn't even discern between north and south, let alone know a single soul living in those mountains.

We arrived in our new town in the wee hours of the morning. The temperature difference was astounding and wonderful. I left the stifling 109°F to wake up to brisk mountain air at an astonishing 48°F. The air was crisp, just enough for your ears to feel cold, but not your arms. We had a rental house a quarter the size of the home we'd just sold, but it was enough. Days of unpacking and nights of organizing were ahead of us—okay, that's a lie.

There was no *us* in any of that. My monster went off on an assignment where he was gone for the first two weeks we were there. I had to navigate almost everything alone, and honestly, I was *pissed*. I'd never been upset about being left alone before. I had grown to love it because I felt so safe when I was alone. This time, I was so ridiculously out of my element. We lived over 90 minutes from the closest grocery store that our bank account could sustain. We were in the thickest, most beautiful mountains I'd ever had the privilege of exploring. I knew no one, and neither did my children. I wanted to get them involved in the community as quickly as possible, but how does one just... *do* that?

I'd decided that I wasn't going to homeschool them any longer. In my research, I discovered that most of the faculty at the *only* elementary school in our new town were all seizure first aid trained. I felt safe that perhaps it was time to let go of the reins a little bit, and perhaps I could go back to writing. So, within a week of living there, I enrolled them in their new school, months before I needed to.

The fast-paced city life I was used to showed with each step I took. I must have looked ridiculous to them in my Chucks and ripped jeans. These were mountain folk of the highest caliber, and I had a hard time making friends as it was.

But you know what? Walking into that school, I fell in complete love. The staff were not only friendly, but they were inviting! They asked questions that mattered to me and made my children feel invincible. The principal listened to my concerns and assured me that at *his* school, my children would not only be safe but they would be seen. He also talked to me about a summer camp that would take place in the following weeks and suggested I enroll the kids there so they could make some friends before school started. *Brilliant!* I thought.

Thank you, God. This is what we needed.

After approximately two months of living in the tiniest of houses (that I grew to LOVE), my monster wanted to upgrade our status. After all, he was one of the elites now. You know in old westerns, when the new sheriff comes to town, they walk around wielding their golden star like they were sent there by God Himself to bring order to the degenerates who'd lived there their whole lives? That was my monster. But more on that later.

He wanted to buy a house. He didn't like the thought of being governed by a landlord or property management company. He wanted to be the king of his own castle. But the options were slim. Our budget was small, though we had a decent down payment in hand because of the sale of our house. No house worked for me; I was screaming on the inside with each one we looked at. He was willing to spend more money than we had, wanted to live where we had property, and did not care how isolated we were. He constantly mentioned how he wanted to keep us safe and away from the view of the outside world. Given his job and the types of people I was told we were living around, I understood it. But I just wanted to settle down where I could grow old in the life I was left to suffer in.

We found a house that had a wraparound porch with more square footage than the place we were renting. The home itself was dark, heavy, and awkward. It oozed with complications and frustrating dynamics. The master bedroom sported one of those accordion doors—the ones you'd see separating rooms at an old church—that stood between the room and the living room. It was brought to our attention sometime later that the previous owners would host massive parties that, well, invited *everyone* into their bedroom.

Great. We nabbed the swingin' party house.

And to add to the weirdness?

The previous owners were still on the property... *buried* on the property.

I laughed a lot. The irony was not lost on me that we were about to purchase a home filled with sex and death. I know it sounds sardonic, but I couldn't (and still cannot) help myself.

The property was beautiful despite the home itself. I love trees and deep forests, and once we moved in, I found myself living amongst both. The brutality of the cold, crisp air was a relief for my bones, but most especially for my mind. I found that I was waking earlier each morning to have a few extra moments to myself—enjoying a cup of tea while I overlooked the creek that roared, breaking the silence of the forest. I felt uneasy within the walls, but I did what I could to make it a home as quickly as possible.

The children started school and were excelling by October. They'd made friends, often riding their bikes with the closest neighbors we had down our mountainous dirt road. The school was a dream come true for us, though. That was another gift I couldn't deny since we had moved. I was grateful.

I felt my shoulders release tension, little by little each day. Was I smiling? Really smiling? I wasn't sure I could trust it, but it sure felt like smiling. My monster was gone more than he was home, and I wasn't feeling the pressure to be some cookie-cutter soccer mom. New manuscripts were pouring from my fingers while the children were at school. I'd landed my second agent, who felt I had all the potential in the world to change the writing industry with my stories. I was solely focused on the good, and that felt incredible.

ARE you waiting for me to say that a shoe was about to drop on my new-found happiness? You must know my story pretty well, then.

Because, of course, there was another shoe.

In the life of a severely abused human being, there's always another shoe waiting to drop. We are plagued with that curse, and the amount of distrust built in our spines means we cannot create a truly happy life.

In my case, the other shoe began to hurl itself in my direction months prior when my sibling asked me to officiate at their wedding.

DISCLAIMER: In recent months, my sibling has proudly come out as non-Binary. I am *immensely* proud of them and will support them with every fiber of my being. That being said, during this time in our lives, they had not come out yet, as they were uncomfortable doing so. That is and was their right. But because I am telling this story rather linearly and because the gender they identified with at the time is very much a point of contention between my abuser and myself, let it be known that I will be using pronouns my sibling no longer identifies with. This was their past and is no longer their present or future. Please be respectful of all humans and refer to them the way they feel most valued and seen.

To my sibling, I respect you, and I love you. Thank you for allowing me to use this part of my story, though the pronouns no longer serve you. I always have been and forever will be your biggest fan. I love you.

—Your Seeester

11

"Sometimes fear does not subside and you must do it afraid."

— ELISABETH ELLIOT

"ARE YOU FUCKING KIDDING ME?"

"Sir, he's my brother. He's asking me to do him a great honor. Please—"

"Absolutely not. They aren't Christians—what do they even want you to say? Let me guess, they don't want Scriptures, and they don't want you to pray?"

"I wouldn't think so, Sir. But love is love, so what does it matter?"

"There you go with that liberal bullshit—Bethany, what did I say? The answer is no. His fiancée is trash anyway. And besides, women shouldn't ever perform a wedding ceremony. It's not their place, and God hates it."

"Sir, it's my brother's wedd—"

"I SAID NO. Do you need to be bound and gagged? Oooh, you know I'll do it. His crap fiancée could have asked you to be a bridesmaid, and I'd still say no because I don't trust her."

"Yes, Sir."

My first and most defiant decision in our marriage was made in that instant. I *would* be the officiant for my baby brother—the one I'd loved more than myself each day since the moment he was laid in my arms on my second birthday. I absolutely would be there for him. I had no clue how I would do it because my brother lived out of state, and I knew the finances alone would never allow it, but I wasn't going to let my monster stop me.

Cut to when we moved, and the topic had to come back up again because I had to buy my dress and shoes. I chose a night when my monster was in a glorious mood. We had more money than we knew what to do with because the sale of our previous home and the purchase of the new home left us with a little nest egg. When I asked, he rolled his eyes. He told me that maybe he'd allow it because we had moved closer to where my brother and soon-to-be sister-in-law lived. He wasn't thrilled with the idea of me performing the ceremony, but I had been "such a good girl," he couldn't see why his opinions should matter.

I wanted to scream in elation. I wanted to call my brother and tell him it was a yes, but the truth was, my brother had no idea there was even a conflict. I knew he hated my monster. I knew my monster hated him. But I didn't want my brother to know how bad I had it at home, especially when it came to anything my brother did.

About a year before my mom was lost, found, and dead, my brother moved in with us briefly. It must have been the biggest torture for him because my monster stood for everything my brother fought against: government, control, misogyny, etc. My brother had no clue that it was torture for me, too. I was punished for every night he stayed in our home. And sometimes, it was humiliating because I was almost positive my brother could hear what was happening in our bedroom. I think I was desperate for my brother to notice and to say something to me about it, but I couldn't expect that of him. He was a young man battling his own demons at the time. I needed to be his place of refuge, though I felt I was anything but that. When my brother moved out suddenly, I knew... I knew our home was a toxic environment that he could not handle. It didn't matter; he was off to safety.

Fast forward to wedding preparations: I wrote the most beautiful ceremony that I could have hoped to have written. I was thrilled. I quoted the Beatles instead of the Bible. I ran with an outpouring of hope, sincerity, and the importance of holding one another in beautiful and good mental health. My monster didn't want to read it, of course, but I was happy. I had to drive out of state to my brother's apartment about two days before my monster and children had to be there. My monster allowed me to rent a car and drive by myself. He was excited about "going camping" with our kids on our property and said he couldn't wait to have a mini road trip with them.

Shock wasn't exactly the word I'd use for how I felt, but I didn't want to focus on it too much. I wanted to GO.

The morning I was to leave, we got into a massive fight. He had changed his mind, echoing the same ridiculousness he'd spewed before.

"You aren't going."

"Why??"

"Why, WHAT? I know I've gone soft on you, but so help me; you'll answer me correctly."

"Why, *Sir*? My brother is counting on me, and we already have the rental car."

"It's complete bullshit. You must be up to something because this isn't like you. Since when do you think this kind of shit is okay? Women should NOT perform wedding ceremonies."

"I'm not up to anything, Sir. I want to be there for my

brother. You and the kids will be meeting me in two days, and—"

"AND THEN WE'RE WHAT, BETHANY? I'M PAYING FOR A GODDAMN HOTEL ROOM I WON'T GET TO ENJOY?"

This went on for a few minutes longer when I did the bravest thing I'd done in our eleven-year marriage:

I walked out the door, got into the rental car, and drove away.

I screamed. I couldn't turn back, but I was in a full-sweat panic over the kids. Why was I married to a man that only made life insufferably difficult? Why was *everything* a controversy or the subject of constant questioning? What was marriage even about if not to love and support one another in each other's hopes and dreams?

It shouldn't be this hard.

By the time I had driven down the mountainside and into better cell service, my phone rang. My monster was yelling profanities I dare not repeat. He was going to leave me; he was going to find someone else. I had crossed the line, and I was going to pay.

After a while, he ran out of steam. He hung up on me and called back a few times, and I suppose he'd lost his fire. He told me he disapproved of my choices, but since my mind was made up, he would have to deal with me later. His tone changed a couple of hours later when the kids returned from school, and he seemed elated to spend the one-on-one time with them. I spoke to my oldest, who echoed the same excitement. My shoulders relaxed. I turned my music up and enjoyed the hell out of the freedom. Seven hours of driving alone. It was a new frontier.

The time I spent with my brother was a dream. He took me around his city—I even rode on a public bus for the first time in my life! We walked, we talked, we laughed, and we caught up without either one of us looking over our shoulders for the wretched man who was my husband. At a point, my brother turned to me and said, "I've missed you."

My soul screamed from within, but I bit my tongue. I knew if I told him what I'd been through, what I was going through at that very moment, I would ruin his wedding. I couldn't do that to my precious brother. He was overjoyed to have his people coming to celebrate his marriage. I chose to rejoice with him and fight with my monster via text behind my brother's back.

I am not a good liar. That is a quality about myself I both covet and despise at the same time. I've had to learn small coping mechanisms to skirt around bold-faced lying to people, and it is not something I am proud of. However, I've also learned that when my level of stress has exceeded my brain's ability to forewarn the outcome of any situation, I tend to get scrambled, and I mix my lies up. It's embarrassing.

A great example is when I was sitting in the back seat as my soon-to-be sister-in-law drove my brother and me to the wedding venue for the rehearsal. My monster was texting me obscenities, angry that I wasn't available to talk to him at that precise moment. I pleaded for him to stop because I didn't want to be rude to my brother and his fiancée.

In response to him telling me he wasn't going to come to the wedding (which meant I would not see my children either) and it was my fault, I responded with:

> I'm sorry, Sir. Please don't be angry with me. I'll take my punishment for my misbehavior. I'm sorry I can't answer the phone right now. I'm so, so sorry. I promise there's no one else. I'm in the car and can't talk. I'm sorry, Sir.

He didn't text me back, but my phone buzzed.

> Umm, who are you calling "Sir" like that, honey?

My bones froze. A wave of panic of the most epic proportions swept over me; I thought I was going to die.

> Bethany?

It wasn't my monster... it was my father.

I had accidentally texted MY FATHER. And now he's asking who the hell I'm talking to like that, or who on earth I was calling "Sir." Like the Grinch, I had to think of a lie, and I had to think of one quick.

> Sorry, Pops, that wasn't meant for you. Laura and I are going back and forth with quotes from a movie we like. That's all it was—no worries. Sorry about that!

He accepted the answer, and when I saw him a couple of hours later, he acted as if the conversation had never happened. *Thank you, God, for an unobservant father.*

I was in the middle of getting a mani/pedi with my brother, his fiancée, and one of my brother's groomsmen—who was a friend of his since high school and was also... a woman. My monster showed up at the nail salon and had my sweet babies with him. They had so many stories of all the fun they'd been having with their daddy. Hugging them relaxed my heart and eased all the mounted tension in my shoulders, if only for a moment. I hadn't told my monster that my brother was also there getting his nails done, and I definitely didn't tell him about the less-than-traditional wedding party.

He snatched me out of the salon as quickly as he could and spoke every bit of his mind all the way to the hotel.

I often wonder what was going through my children's minds at moments like that. Their daddy, who had been their unabashed hero while they spent special time with him, turned into an outraged psycho beast at the sight of their mother. I wonder if angels guarded their young minds or if they simply learned that you treat your spouse that way. As time has gone on, I can promise you it was the former because they cannot recall any such conversations or interactions.

The wedding was beautiful. My brother and his new bride had gone to extreme lengths to make their nuptials storybook perfect. I sobbed when I pronounced them married and introduced them to the crowd as my brother and new sister. I danced with my children and my grandmother in her walker. I spent time with my cousins, whom I did not often see. I tried to have fun while I could because I knew the long drive home was ahead of me in the morning.

"HE TOOK HER LAST NAME? WHAT A PUSSY! He's not a man, Bethany. I don't know if I want him around our kids!"

Ladies and gentlemen, I would love to tell you that I stood up for my brother. I would love to say that I fought like hell and made my monster see that I would always put my own flesh and blood before my own well-being. I wish I could. My brother deserved that much because Lord knows I loved him and 100% supported his choices. But I was tired. I was deep-in-my-bones tired and couldn't handle arguing for over seven hours of driving. I spit out a lie that made me sick, a lie that still burns in my heart of ashes...

"I know, Sir. I think I've lost him forever."

As I type this—almost a decade later—I am bawling. This was a tragic death for me, my emotional state, and the relationship I'd sworn to God to protect, all in the name of survival. I don't know if it's right or normal to feel like wanting to live to see my children grow is excuse enough not to sacrifice myself for someone who mattered to me. I don't know if that's a predestined thought put in my brain from birth by my martyr of a mother or if that's a trauma response. Either way, from that point forward and out of survival, I formed an unspoken bond with my abuser that betrayed my heart.

My sibling was born four days shy of my second birthday. I have loved them fiercely from the moment they were placed in my lap. I would bend the earth in half if they asked me to. I would abandon my dreams if they needed me. There is no length too far that I would go to ensure or guarantee their happiness. That being said, the ultimate sin I committed against my sibling sent me spiraling mentally. I felt like I was slowly sinking to my death, like I was trapped in a tar pit, never to escape.

A statement like that went a long way in my monster's mind. Not only did we not fight on the way home, but we wound up stopping at one of the biggest outdoorsy/sporting goods stores (a bucket list item for him, as there were none anywhere close to where we lived), and he bought me a $200 winter jacket so that I could survive living in our new mountain town.

I felt disgusting. I felt cheap. I felt like the ultimate betrayer, someone who should never be forgiven. To this day, I still haven't forgiven myself. My sibling has no clue about any of this, and I hope that they can forgive me if they ever discover what I did.

I HAVE a lot to be sorry for during those years; I have a lot I will never be able to come to terms with because I cannot fathom where my backbone went. But that's abuse. That's what being a victim is. You might be shaking your head in disbelief because nothing I'm saying can resonate with you.

There's also a chance you might be nodding your head in agreement. You might be cut to the quick because you get it, and it kills you. There's nothing like it, is there? That sense of loss, that sense of worthlessness because you've allowed someone to rip your heart out of you and closed you off to the things you were once passionate about?

That's abuse.

No, you aren't bleeding. No, you don't have broken bones or bruises.

But friends, I assure you—that loss of self, that pain, that hollow feeling within you caused by another person's "rules?" That's abuse. And you don't deserve it.

So, somewhere within you—somewhere within me— forgiveness of self must be found.

But we'll come back to that.

AFTER WE ARRIVED HOME, I faced cleaning up the mess my monster and children left from their two nights without me. Despite my exhaustion, I did the dishes, cleaned the kitchen, packed up the tent they used for camping, and threw away all their trash.

When I lifted the lid on the garbage can, something shiny caught my eye: something tucked away in an empty cardboard box.

A beer can.

My monster was drinking again.

12

"Pain shapes a woman into a warrior."

— R.H. SIN

THE MOST WONDERFUL TIME OF THE YEAR IS NOT CHRISTMAS FOR me. Don't get me wrong, I am just as obsessed with the twinkling lights and watching Clark Griswold turn into a perpetual madman, all for the sake of having a "good old-fashioned family Christmas," as much as the next guy. But my favorite season is October.

*Bethany, October isn't a **season**.*

Oh, but it is to me! The leaves are in the middle of their final dance of the year, changing colors and adorning the earth with magic. The air is crisp but not cold enough to suffer. October brings bonfires and darker afternoons. But best of all, October brings... Halloween.

I have loved Halloween since I can remember, and anyone who knows me personally can say without a doubt how true that is. It's the spooky, the macabre, the imagination, and the atmosphere that makes Halloween a place I can always escape to.

If I could live in an old Victorian mansion with its steep gabled roof and turrets and towers, I would. Obsessively. Give me the sensational dormers, dripping with stained glass and details that cannot be recreated "these days." I would walk around adorned with a crow on my shoulder and stacks of books in each corner of every room. I would write poetry and sip tea on dark days.

Oh yes, that's who resides in this heart of mine!

October of 2015 was something magical on its own, at least outside.

Living among the forest of evergreen trees meant darkness came early every day. I couldn't get enough of sitting and writing by the woodstove, blazing with a fire warm enough to last us through the night, while the children were at school and my monster was at work. I decorated the house exquisitely, in the most perfect and haunted fashion. I made a graveyard out front (not to be confused with the *actual* graveyard this house came with) that looked as real as possible. I focused every effort on finding my happiness in the details, the cool weather, and the denial.

Denial? What denial?

My husband was drinking again, but he was hiding it from me. Growing up the daughter of an addict, I knew this dance, and I knew it well. He was angrier, he was uptight, and the little things were making him snap. When I confronted my monster about the beer can in the trash, he explained that they'd found it on the property and thrown it away. Considering where we lived, it was a plausible explanation because people often hiked around our property and discarded or dumped their trash. Annoying, yes, so I accepted the possibility and moved on.

But oh, this gift of discernment I have.

I couldn't help but get the sense that something was off. I had felt this feeling many times before, each time I caught him in a big lie. That first time when I discovered chewing tobacco? Felt it. The time I found he'd purchased pornography just after learning he'd be a father? Felt it. The multitudes of times after that with both of those issues *and* the times that didn't add up when he was gone on assignment? FELT. IT.

I get that feeling a lot, even now, with my own children. It's like a honing beacon that I can't move past. I know I'm exceedingly intuitive, but this feels more psychic, and there's no other way to describe it.

While my monster was at work and my children were at school, I prayed, just like I always did when I got that sick feeling in my heart:

Show me. What is he hiding? Help me to see it CLEARLY so he cannot deny it. Help me to see exactly what this feeling is and help me know what to do and say when I discover the truth. Amen

As soon as I opened my eyes from my prayer, I had the overwhelming sensation of checking inside his car. I had no clue what I was looking for; I just knew to go inside and focus on the backseat.

I was terrified and felt silly. I was never wrong, but I wanted to believe I was. I wanted to believe I was paranoid—just like I was always told. But I wasn't.

On the floorboard behind the driver's seat was a crumbled receipt.

Am I really THAT woman right now??

I may have opened it slowly, or with fervent speed, I can't recall. My heart was in my throat in either case.

The receipt was from the local grocery store. The date was October 2, 2015—the day I left for the wedding. It had a few items on it: ingredients for making dinner and s'mores, a four-pack of specialty root beer that the kids loved, and... two 12-packs of beer.

Fire burned within me. I felt the adrenaline rush down from the top of my head, run hot through my cheeks, encapsulate my chest, and spread to my hands and feet. I fought all my immediate urges for swift justice, so I did not call him. I took a picture of the receipt (just in case) and slowly made my way to my favorite spot on our oversized deck. I watched the creek bubble and race swiftly down the mountainside, weighing my few options. I could ignore it, as that receipt was from a few weeks ago. I could confront him and risk a big blow-up, or I could... I didn't know. I was just so desperate for my life to be happy. I *was* happy in the mountains, amongst the trees, watching my children blossom in school and with friends. But that "*but;*" made all those wonderful things feel like dandelion wishes amid a hurricane.

I decided to do a little more investigative work before I confronted him. I did not want to be fueled by confused or conflicting emotions. I was 30 years old, dang it. I could handle this, approach this like the freaking adult I was.

I picked up my children from school and took them to our favorite little market. I was a big fan of rewarding their hard-earned school week by doing something I called "Junk Food Friday." The deal was that they would eat healthy all week, do their chores, and get their schoolwork done, and come Friday, I would buy them treats and pizza to enjoy. Occasionally, we loved getting shaved ice, and we would sit together and talk about our favorite parts of the week.

This time, I had an ulterior motive.

Once we had our shaved ice, we sat at our favorite table and began to talk. I asked my oldest if they could remember what camping with Daddy was like when I was gone that week. They said it was a lot of fun but that Daddy fell asleep fast because he was tired. I asked if they got any special treats while they were camping. My youngest shouted, "We got S'MORES, and they were deeeeeelicious!" We all laughed.

I pressed one last time. I didn't want to lead the conversation; I wanted it to feel organic and free from pressure.

"Did you guys get any special drinks?"

"We got root beers, Mommy! And they were goo-ood!" My youngest, ever the comedian.

"That's wonderful! Did Daddy drink root beer, too? He's not the biggest root beer fan, I know. So, it would mean that was some pretty special root beer if he did!"

My oldest looked down at the table and did not make eye contact.

"Daddy had... regular beer."

I clenched my jaw. My suspicions were not only confirmed but I had been told that he drank until he passed out ("Daddy fell asleep because he was tired") and that something about it made my oldest not want to tell me. I changed the subject quickly with an "Okie dokie, kiddo! So, tell me about recess today! Did you play ball-wall?"

How would you approach this? You know your spouse is supposed to be sober because he became physically violent with you and was arrested for it. You know they drank when you weren't around once; do you question if they've been drinking at other times? Do you leave the information where it lies and pretend you never learned any of it?

I was at a crossroads I didn't want to freaking be at. And remember, I am *not* a good liar. I am also one for justice and do not want any inequity to go unrecognized or unresolved. I had to decide not *if* I would confront him but *how*.

He came home that night. The kids were already in bed when I greeted him at the door. I took a deep breath, reminding myself I had prayed for proof. I was given the proof for a reason.

It must have meant I would come out on the other side safe and sound.

After he changed out of his uniform, I put together our dinners and set them on the coffee table in front of the television. On his utensils, I placed the receipt. When he sat down, I made sure I was fumbling about the kitchen, getting drinks or something.

I held my breath, waiting for the outrage that was surely coming. I hadn't even noticed that I'd overfilled my cup with water, spilling out onto the counter. The silence exploded in my ears. I rounded the corner of the living room, unsure what to expect.

He was holding the receipt and was... crying.

"I'm sorry, Bethany. I'm so sorry."

For a brief moment, I thought I was being filmed secretly for some popular prank TV show. I remember literally looking over my shoulder in dismay and concern. Why was he crying? Was this real? Was he about to fly off the handle, and this was the last moment I would breathe air?

No. He sat there, head in hands, crying.

And this time, *I* was filled with rage.

"After everything we've been through? After *all* the therapy and all the moments we've spent trying to heal and get away from 2013? You did *this*? In front of *our kids*?! What's wrong with you?!"

He stopped crying. Anger ignited in his eyes. I didn't fall for his tears, so there was no use in pretending they served a purpose. He shouted at me that it was my fault, that I had driven him to drink because I refused to obey him about going to my brother's wedding. If I had just followed his rules and listened to him, he wouldn't have fallen off the wagon. It was *my* fault.

And so was 2013.

Oh, friends, how tired I was of hearing that. We fought about his first arrest so often I had the entire thing memorized. His abuse and arrest had happened over two years prior. I was still getting blamed as we rehashed every detail time and time again. I was to blame. I was always to blame.

As he yelled at me, he let slip that the campout with the kids was not the first time he'd had a drink since his arrest. I didn't let that go. What did he mean? How much had he been lying? Wait a second... I was spinning.

While I was back in our cookie-cutter home, trying to sell it, homeschool the kids, live life as a full-time single mother, battling my depression, and putting every ounce of energy I had into making our family function and operate correctly, he was living in the barracks and drinking. And drinking some more. And basically, living like a single man. Now, he swore up and down that he never cheated on me. He swore he was miserable, and if I had just sold the house faster, he wouldn't have been forced to be lonely. He wouldn't have had a single thing to drink. It was my fault.

It shouldn't be this hard.

We went to bed as the sun came up. I was exhausted from having my guts ripped from my body and laid before me once again. I had no interest in justice. I'd given up. I was done. I served no purpose other than to make sure my children made it into adulthood and to be a hole for my monster to fill when he was in the mood. I was useless. I was a waste of space.

I didn't understand why God put me on this earth because what good was I? Was I God's court jester? That would have described me perfectly. Perhaps I was created so that God had something to make Him chuckle. I was the modern-day female equivalent of Job, the man who suffered his whole life because Satan wanted to prove that he could persuade Job to lose his faith in God. I felt like I was walking in Job's sandals. I had to swallow those feelings and move on, though. I had stopped writing in my journal years before, but looking back, I know I would have done better mentally if I'd kept writing. I was worried about him reading my journals, so I kept *all* my thoughts inside my head where they were safe. A day would come when I could say everything. There'd be a day I was safe.

The following few months were met with stress but intention. My monster went to great lengths to show me he wasn't drinking. He was also doing his best to remain present and be involved in his family's life. His ego at work was something else, and I was uneasy about it. We'd made friends with other law enforcement families and tried to fit in where we could. I sensed no one liked my monster, but I couldn't prove it.

Christmas came and went, bringing my father and his fiancée up for an awkward visit. I was obsessed with the feet upon feet of snow we continued to get all winter, and I began the journey to live holistically and be a plastic-free household. My freedom in the kitchen and house was my sanctuary, so being trapped inside due to the climate wasn't the worst thing. I think my father thought I was slipping into madness with all of that, but he didn't utter a word.

We ushered in 2016 with hope and excitement.

And maybe you don't believe in karma, but this girl saw it prevail that year.

13

"She's fire
But she won't burn you...
she knows all too well,
how it feels to live with ashes."

— ALFA

IF THERE WERE CHAPTERS I WAS LOOKING FORWARD TO WRITING, IT would be the next two. Not because I'm a glutton for revenge or because 2016 was easy on me. Rather, I wasn't the focus of my monster's anger for once. It brought a time when the man who had laughed in my face for years, claiming my mental health issues were fake and that my two suicide attempts were just me looking for attention, *finally* understood what it meant to want to die.

But let's start with my father's wedding that May.

Unlike my brother's wedding, I wasn't asked to do anything "controversial" in my father's nuptials. He had a traditional Scottish handfasting ceremony in the most beautiful backyard I had ever seen. There was lush grass, a never-ending property, and one of the biggest sweeping willows that I couldn't take my eyes off. We had traveled the nearly nine-hour trip, and I did all I could to make myself as busy as possible, leaving little for anyone to talk to me about. I just wasn't in the mood. My monster was obsessed with talking crap about his captain, and the negativity thwarted all efforts to enjoy myself.

I wanted to be happy for my father. I rather enjoyed his fiancée and looked forward to getting to know her better. I did everything I was supposed to, even spending time with his fiancée's teenage daughter and adult sons. I went and got my nails done with them, kept my smile strong, and stayed away from the guilt I felt about my mother. It was odd; I felt like not only condoning but also being present for my father's wedding was somehow a betrayal of my mother's love. She hadn't even been dead for three years. But also, my parents had been separated from one another for over 11 years—so not even I understood my pain.

Perhaps I was just tired. That's what I told myself. I was tired. I missed my family, and I was allowing my exhaustion to interfere with the time I could have been spending with them.

Enough, Bethany. Enough.

The wedding was fairytale-worthy. My children, my brother, and his wife each added elements to my father and his bride's handfasting cord, and I got to drape and pin our family's tartan over my new stepmother as a sign of bringing her into the family. I was more than happy that my monster was left out of the ceremony entirely. I never asked my father if that was done intentionally, but it brought me great joy.

They were married, and it was party time.

And party we did.

Being a Scottish family means that when celebrations occur, whisky flows like rain out of the sky. I'll be honest and say that I absolutely let myself go. I was in a safe environment and felt I deserved to enjoy myself. I danced with my babies, my cousins, and my uncles. I had a ball. And then my heart was shredded.

Two things happened at the exact same time that made me realize no matter how hard I tried, I couldn't mean as much to my father as I needed to, and I could not ever win the battle of alcoholism within my monster.

When I was nine, I was in Girl Scouts. Did I love Girl Scouts? Absolutely not. I wanted to be in Cub Scouts with my brother, but that wasn't allowed. Anyway, in Girl Scouts, there was a Daddy/Daughter dance my mother forced me to attend. My father tried to make it all cute by bringing me a bouquet of flowers and a corsage. We posed in front of the fireplace while my mom took pictures—he in his suit and me in my brand-new cream-colored dress. It felt like... a date. It was uncomfortable, and I couldn't put my finger on why.

At the dance, there were hundreds of bored-looking fathers with their uptight, snotty daughters. I didn't have any friends there, so I couldn't escape the awkwardness I felt. My father looked uncomfortable, too, but it's possible that was my nine-year-old perception. He kept asking if I wanted to dance, but I absolutely did not. It felt... wrong.

Eventually, guilt took over for me. I knew my father had spent money on me, the event, the flowers, and dinner. I knew I should dance with him at least once.

Funny enough, a song came on that I happened to love at the time. It was a country song that was fast enough, so I knew I wouldn't have to face the discomfort that slow dancing would bring for me. The song was "Ain't Goin' Down ('Til the Sun Comes Up)" by Garth Brooks.

Listen, I am fully aware *now* of how inappropriate that song is, but that's what we danced to. And you know what? It wasn't half bad. I remember laughing and feeling pretty cool because when he would spin me, my long skirt did the proper princess twirl. The night was salvaged in my mind, a memory I look back on and smile.

All that to say, that song became a staple—an inside bonding moment for the two of us. It was perhaps the only one we ever had, honestly. When my monster and I were married, I surprised my father by playing that song as our father/daughter dance. My father had no clue that I remembered and wept when I grabbed the microphone to make the announcement and gave the much-needed explanation to the crowd. So, when it came time for *his* wedding, I made sure to sneak that song on the playlist.

Now, to the part where my heart was shattered by two incidents that happened simultaneously.

The guy in charge of hitting "play" on the iPod told me that the song I had requested was coming up. So, I asked my monster to record my father's reaction and the two of us dancing together. When the song came on, I went out to the dance floor. I waited eagerly. I searched the crowd but couldn't find my father. He was nowhere in sight. I called to my oldest child to find their grandfather. Even my new stepmother knew the importance of that song, so she went looking for him, too. I felt like a fool, standing there waiting. I looked to my right and saw my monster —who was not recording or even holding my phone—chug a beer.

Stood up by my father, and my monster couldn't resist a drink.

I was crushed.

Turns out my father was as wasted as I'd ever seen him. He couldn't remember my name, let alone remember that our song had played. But, hey... it was his wedding. Who was I to get wounded like that?

We packed up the next day and started our long journey back home. It was about to be busy season for my monster, so I got to hear all about his plans for the different operations and how he would focus on staying out of his captain's line of sight. We didn't argue; we didn't even have tension. I chose not to mention that he drank because he did not mention me being disrespectful or any of the typical accusations.

The month went on, and the last week of school activities commenced. I volunteered at my children's amazing school as often as I could so the community was learning to accept our family fully. That week was no exception. On the last day of school, they had "Field Day," where all the elementary students participated in dozens of outdoor group activities. I helped for a few hours and was elated to see how happy my babies were. Maybe this move was the best choice for them after all.

On my way home, my monster called. Something had happened, and he was worried he was in trouble.

Legally, I cannot state what happened. But I *can* say that he was accused of making a false arrest. The way he explained his side of the story, it seemed he didn't do anything wrong. But according to his captain—the one he claimed was *always* rude to him—he did. And because of it, my monster was put on paid leave pending an investigation.

What did that mean? It meant that my monster was home-bound. It meant that he wouldn't be able to go on assignments or bring in all that overtime money that summer. Oh, it meant so much agony.

He went through the stages of grief like I've never seen another soul do. He did not believe that what was happening to him could be happening to him. He called everyone he knew to prove his innocence. He would not stop talking about how unfair his punishment was. And to be honest, the punishment didn't fit the crime. Something wasn't adding up for sure.

His anger was exemplary, from physically punishing his body during workouts to throwing large tree limbs around the property and bellowing profanities at God. He walked around our home like a caged lion. There was no rest. There was no peace. He remodeled both of the house's bathrooms and built me a beautiful table for the deck, but only to distract himself. He would go through fits of rage at me, the children, and random strangers in stores. He was explosive and terrifying. I understood because I'm not sure I'd feel differently. He loved his job more than he loved anything else. It was his status. It was what made him better than all the rest. And his fury was fueled when other law enforcement officers, including his very own partner, did not aid him.

My "spidey senses" began to tingle after about three months of this. There was no word from his captain or even the union representative assigned to my monster and his case. I couldn't help but wonder if, perhaps, my monster had, in fact, done something wrong. *Very* wrong.

His bargaining phase was an absolute nightmare. This is where he looked the weakest to me. Did I hate it? Well, that's a tough question. My conscious self felt sorry for him. Of course, I would. He was still the man I was married to; I still loved him in the only way I knew to love him. He wasn't punishing me sexually at that time (though the threats had increased tenfold), but he was moping around like I'd never seen. He almost seemed *normal*. My subconscious self was elated. Whenever I went to the store alone or did laundry without his eye on me, I smiled. I smiled big. And maybe that is the wrong or inappropriate response. However, my oh-so-human side couldn't help but feel like justice was being served a little. That maybe, somehow, he would see how important I was: that he couldn't function without all the things I did, that I really did work hard to run the household, that I was an honest-to-God good woman.

His bargaining led to depression in big ways. He'd run around asking for favors, asking for company, and promising that if others would help him, he'd be willing to do anything. His bargaining did not lead to deeper friendships or kind responses. Even our closest friends, our neighbors with four wonderful kids, were awkward around us. What more could we say? Something was up. They knew it, I knew it. But my monster refused. His depression was not something I was equipped to handle anymore. After years and years of being told that depression isn't real and that people want an easy out because they can't "man up" or "woman up" and face their problems, I didn't know what to say. I didn't know how to be the empath, the listener, or the helper I was created to be. I'd lost my words somewhere in the caves of my broken soul, and in the end, he suffered because of it.

My monster woke up crying. He went to bed crying. After a while, I didn't know what else to do. This chaos, this life change, had completely uprooted our family, our poor children, and I was running around trying to be everyone's savior. At a point, my monster admitted to putting his gun in his mouth and crying out to God to stop him.

Guys, when he told me that, I almost booked an immediate appointment for myself with a therapist... a priest... or maybe even a ticket straight to hell.

I still think about it because the thought that ran across my mind was horrendous.

But would you blame me?

14
———

"Your purpose is hidden within your wounds."

— RUNE LAZULI

I WANT YOU TO PUT YOURSELF IN MY SHOES: LET'S SAY YOU WERE married to someone who had been so emotionally and mentally abusive to you for over 12 years, and no matter what you'd done —even when he was arrested for getting incredibly violent with you—he was still roaming free. What would your reaction be if that person told you that they just wanted to end it all and that they got close to doing it?

Mine was not something I'm proud of.

I went into the bathroom and flipped God off.

Why, God? Why didn't You let him go? Yes, it would have been trau-matic, and I have no clue how I would have handled it, but DAMN IT. We could have been free!

See what I mean? I should have committed myself or confessed to a holy man or *something* because that was a very ugly thing to think. But Lord Almighty... the little revenge demon within me was upset the gun did not fire.

Of course, I hugged him. I loved on him. I embraced the face that had spit so many profanities and ugly defamations in mine, even when I was at my lowest. I did what I vowed to do: to be his wife for better or worse.

My monster hung on to depression for quite a few months. All the while, he was still getting little to no information about the charges, when he could go back on duty, or if he should start looking for other employment.

We began to train, as a family, to run a Spartan race. It became our obsession. Working together, challenging each other, and looking forward to each day with one another truly did help. It seemed that by August, he'd come out of his depression and was in the beginning stages of acceptance. He seemed nicer, calmer, even. I had been previously booked to attend a huge conference for the Society of Children's Book Writers and Illustrators (SCBWI). I was a Co-Assistant Regional Advisor for our area's chapter (this is a well-respected international society for all writers and illustrators of children's books), and part of my duties was to attend conferences. He had permitted me to go as long as I found someone to spend the weekend with our children. In March of that year, before all the madness with my monster's job occurred, I had agreed with my father that I would drive the kids to his house and continue to the conference. All in all, it would be a 12-hour drive for me.

Though my monster wasn't working when it came time for my trip, I did not want to leave my children with him. So, I kept to the original plan, telling my monster it would be good for him to spend some time alone. He could reconnect with himself and spend time with God.

The plan worked.

My God, I had the best time! My children were safe with my

father and his wife, and I was safe in an *enormous* hotel suite all by myself in one of the most haunted hotels in America. This suite had two doors (a mud room, of sorts), a solid steel enclosed shower, a clawfoot bathtub, and more square footage than I knew what to do with. Not once had I ever traveled alone, so this was a luxury I wasn't sure how to handle. I was awkward, I was uncomfortable, and I had no clue what to do with my hands—and that was before I'd even left my room!

The writer's conference was incredible, too. I sat and communed with like-minded humans, some of whom I'd met online and become fierce friends. Most of those friends knew my situation with my child (many had donated their books or called to video chat with my baby while they were in the hospital), but none knew about my situation in my marriage.

There was so much freedom to enjoy, but knowing no one knew or would ever guess the life I had waiting for me back home was sheer bliss.

I spoke to *women* without being questioned. I talked to *men* without fear that I was going to be punished. I was a PERSON! A real-life person who could make their own decisions, be responsible, and learn about the industry I was desperate to be a part of. Not to be ridiculously cliché, but I soaked it all in like a freaking sponge. I met, hugged, and chatted with great humans like Henry Winkler, Richard Peck, and a handful of Caldecott winners. I was able to relax, drink with colleagues, laugh, and—dare I say it again? RELAX. My shoulders felt inappropriate resting where they belonged on my body and not in my ears.

I was in heaven for four days, and my time went far too quickly.

I know it goes without saying that my monster called me *often*. Perhaps it was wrong of me, but there were a few times when I claimed I was in meetings when I wasn't. I felt horrible lying to him because I hate lying in general. But that conference was life-affirming, and I was having a blast.

I learned quite a few lessons the hard way. Looking back now, I laugh and laugh at my naïveté. I thought the nice gentlemen in white blazers helping me out of my car each night were just the valets that came free with my stay. Um. No. That was a $58.00 per night mistake I made and had to remedy on my own.

I also learned that I don't like steamed chai, but what I detest even more is telling the barista they got my order wrong. I discovered that underground food courts in the middle of the city are totally my thing.

Friends... I was almost 31 years old, learning these simple, ridiculous truths!

I had never eaten on my own or walked around amongst strangers on my own and had most certainly *never* slept in a hotel room on my own. The turning point of the weekend was when I was invited to go on a stroll "after hours" and do a ghost hunt of the hotel with some writer friends. I was terrified I'd get into trouble and nearly didn't go. But my phone sincerely died. I took that as a sign that I deserved to have extra fun.

With every step I took that weekend, I saw small glimpses of who I still was on the inside. It was rewarding and sickening at the same time. I realized that I truly was as damaged as I feared. I wasn't normal or free like the other women I was around. I wasn't ambitious or feisty like I used to pride myself on being. A well-known and highly respected author spoke to their audience, inspiring everyone by asking, "What is *your* dream? Not your family's dream, not your agent's dream, not your editor's dream, not even your readers' dream. What is *YOUR* dream?"

I... didn't have one.

Was I broken? Surely not, right? Perhaps my mother's

overzealous humility had seeped into my DNA because there was no way I didn't have a... a dream... right?

The fact was, I had no dreams for myself. I wanted to raise my children to be good humans who changed the world with a few of the lessons they learned from me. I wanted them to rise above the noise their generation was sure to throw their way and CONQUER. But... me?

A dream?

The end of the conference arrived, and much like all the kids on the final day of summer camp, there were a few tears. Granted, for some, tears erupted because of the friendships made or the inspiring bumps in self-esteem and ambition. What a gift it was for these brilliantly creative humans to go home, write, draw, or create from their own safe spaces. They were filled with light and joy—the world was their oyster; nothing would stop them.

My tears were different.

I knew what was waiting for me at home. I knew the questions I'd be asked and the berating that would come. I could not wait to hold my children tight and love on them, hearing of their adventures with Grandpa. After the long drive home, I knew I would be in trouble.

You see, I posted a picture on Instagram that I had taken with a famous author/illustrator who was (okay, still *is*) all the rage at the time. I was his helper at his book signing (one of the perks of being on "staff" at this conference). What one must understand about the KidLit world is that most conferences are all but dominated by women. I took several pictures and schmoozed with dozens of delightful ladies with whom I still hold very close to my heart. But that one picture... that one picture was a nail in my coffin.

It was 1,000 percent *the most* awkward picture I have ever taken. Yeah, I was a teensy bit star-struck and was trying not to be a giant dweeb by showing it. But I also knew I wasn't allowed to be around other men, so it was difficult for me to act like a normal human being. To this day, I wonder if this most esteemed gentleman ever wonders what happened to that odd duck of a woman he was forced to be paired with that night in 2016.

I digress.

When I finally arrived home, my monster awaited me on the deck. That big, beautiful deck that I loved with all my heart. The sun was shining through the trees just right. "Look, Bethie, it's *God-light*," my mother would have said. This time, I was too scared to focus on it or see it as a gift. The usual hugs and kisses happened; the children were thrilled to see him. I had already spent nearly 24 hours with them then, so I'd gotten all the updates from Grandpa. But they told their daddy everything and eventually found themselves playing with our dogs and announcing they were ready for dinner.

After the kids' bedtime routine was finished and they were snoring away, my monster asked me to sit with him on the couch. The house was too quiet. Given that he had a beer in his hand, I was terrified.

Calmly, quietly, he stared intently at his beer bottle.

"Sit down," he said slowly as I entered the living room.

Per his rules, I sat, not making eye contact or touching him.

"I am going to ask you one time, and one time only, and then we're going to let this go. Do you understand?"

"Yes, Sir."

I was so tired.

"When you told me you had to go to this conference, you told me it would be mostly women, correct?"

"Yes, Sir. I—"

"No. No, no, no," he whispered, clenching his teeth and beer bottle. "You don't get to speak until I ask you a question. I'm not going to yell. I'm not going to. But I swear to God, if you interrupt me, I will tie you down and whip you so hard. *SO* fucking hard, do I make myself clear?"

"Yes, Sir."

"Now, with all those women at the conference, just tell me one thing, One FUCKING thing. Why did you take a picture with a man?"

Heaven help me. I knew better. What was wrong with me? I. KNEW. BETTER. But I'd posted it, he'd seen it, and now I couldn't even come up with some bizarro lie to save me. I had nothing. I was exhausted and worn out from my travels. There was nothing that was going to save me. He hadn't truly punished me sexually in a long while at that point, but it was coming now. How was I going to gather the strength?

He screamed that I would never be allowed to do anything like that again. He told me I had to quit my volunteer job with SCBWI and that he *knew* I was the whore he figured I was.

"I wasted my time missing you."

"I'm sorry, Sir."

"You will be."

That night was the first time I'd been whipped in a while.

And look, please understand that *everyone* has a kink. I am in no way attempting to make you feel ashamed of yours, as I firmly believe in you... well, doing what *you* like!

You must understand that none of what happened to me in the bedroom was my choice. *If* I was allowed to have an orgasm, I had to ask permission. And when I was whipped with the crop, there were a few times when he drew blood. This was one of those times.

I never went to another writing conference again.

TRIGGER WARNING!

DISCUSSIONS OF SELF-HARM AND SUICIDE UP AHEAD. If you are not in the right headspace, please take your time and wait to go on until you are ready.

YOU ARE LOVED, YOU ARE NEEDED, AND YOU ARE SEEN!

Do not push yourself.

15

"Watch me
    I will go to my own Sun
    And if I am burned by its fire,
    I will fly on scorched wings."

— SEGOVIA AMIL

THE CHANGING OF THE LEAVES MEANT SUMMER WAS OVER, AND THE
routine of school, soccer, and making sure we had enough fire-
wood for the winter was in order. My monster was still
suspended, and his fury was building. He'd lost out on an entire
summer of overtime, adrenaline rushes, and hiding whatever he
would hide from his family.

We were in a tight spot financially, which made things worse.
We'd lost the few friends we'd made because his unrelenting
frustration towards his boss and blame for everyone he'd felt
abandoned by was categorically insane. I would take him to the
little in-store Starbucks when the kids returned to school so that

we could talk. I was trying so hard to be supportive, but God... I was getting tired of talking about it. It was the same conversation over and over again. I had it memorized.

About that time, an interesting offer presented itself to me:

A job.

A real, actual paying job where I could leave the house and be a little independent. A position where I could make money and possibly have some retirement one day.

A job.

Me.

Now, the trick was getting my monster on board. How would I do that? Being a stay-at-home wife and mom was a requirement. It was the quintessential achievement for any God-fearing, traditional man to have a woman at home who takes care of everything while he works and makes money. Life wouldn't exist for that man if not for this woman, but ideally, that woman will never get that kind of credit.

Oops, am I saying too much?

My apologies.

So, attempting to ask my monster's permission was terrifying. From what I can remember (because, believe me, much of this time in my life is now a blur), I tried to present the idea of me having a job to him so that it would ultimately appear to be *his* idea.

I know, ladies, I know. We all laugh and joke about "tricking" our husbands into just about anything by having them believe the idea to do, buy, sell, etc., was all theirs. I distinctly remember learning this little deceitful strategy from Jill Taylor on the '90s TV show "Home Improvement." Well, any '90s TV show, really. That was the common theme back then: Men are stupid. Women are smart. Let's all laugh at the mistakes and tomfoolery the men can get into while the women step in to roll their eyes and save the day.

Yuck.

But I digress... I had to use such a technique for me to have a chance at keeping us afloat. I saw a glimmer of hope just beyond my reach of the darkness we'd been living in that year. I had to try.

I do remember using a moment when he was exceedingly stressed about money.

Chin down. Eyes glued to my shoes.

"Sir, would it help if I got a job? I was offered to work with special needs children at the kids' school. I'd be with [our children] every day, on their schedule, which would save us on gas money. Would that be something that would be helpful?"

He was silent.

I was terrified.

"Are there male teachers there? You know what, never mind. I don't think that would be the worst idea. You'd be around kids and are pretty good with the special ones."

"Yes, Sir."

"You'd still be able to keep up with the house?"

"Of course, Sir."

"Understand that the moment you start slacking around the house is the moment I'm dragging you out of there and bringing your ass home."

"Yes, Sir. I will keep the house clean."

"And none of this, 'My feet are tired, and I can't cook dinner' bullshit, right?"

"No, Sir. I'll be done by 2:30 p.m. every day. I'll be able to do it all just the same as now."

"Good. Go apply."

I had to take a county exam to qualify for the position of Para Educator and go through a couple of interviews, but ultimately, it was an easy ordeal because it was such a small town.

My monster tried to get me in with the Sheriff's Department

first, though, thinking I was safe there and could keep an eye on them if they were talking crap about him. I didn't make it through that grueling interview very well because it was not something I wanted to do.

But after I passed the Para Educator test (with flying colors, I might add), my monster congratulated me and allowed me to orgasm. Yee haw.

As my orientation day approached, my biggest concern was the fresh cuts I had on my forearm. Yeah, can you blame me? I couldn't express my hurt, so I went straight into high-school-Bethany mode and started cutting myself. My monster didn't notice at first, but when we ran up some hills training for our Spartan event, one of the cuts began to bleed. He noticed *that* and immediately asked, "What the fuck did you do?"

Sigh... I lied. Again. It was becoming my go-to habit when it involved my feelings or when I was afraid of punishment. We had a cantankerous cat, you see, and I was quick to blame him.

"Zane got me, Sir. I thought I was being funny and pretended to put him into the pool. I guess I learned a lesson that day."

"I guess you did. Crazy ass woman."

I had to be a little more careful, so I kept reopening the same cuts and blamed my Type 1 Diabetes for the lack of healing. Sick, right? I genuinely thought I was a genius. I was incapable of "normal" thoughts; I felt like I needed an insane asylum. Maybe. There were days when I would watch myself bleed and laugh uncontrollably. Friends, this isn't the mark of a person whose mental health is okay. I had been whittled down to the bare bones of every emotional plane in the universe. I hadn't a thought for myself or my well-being. I just knew I had to keep putting one foot in front of the other. Besides, working at the school would be safe. *I* would be safe.

Orientation day came. I already knew most of the students

and staff I was to work with, which made life much easier. But can I tell you just how ridiculously good it felt to be on my own and making money?! Of course, the money all went to him, but I got to fill out a W-4 in *my* name! I hadn't done that since I was 18 years old. I got to make my own lunches and have my own schedule.

After the first few weeks, I was *in love* with my coworkers and students. I had a purpose, and I got to see my children and understand what they were up to every day. It was a gift for sure, even though it frustrated my monster. All of a sudden, our roles had switched, and he wasn't exactly thrilled about it. He always made snide comments about how I was wearing the pants. Hostility grew as he didn't get the answers he wanted from his union representative. It was a weird time being split between two universes: one where I was incredibly at peace and happy—surrounded by uplifting situations with people who encouraged me daily and with a home life that only made me hate myself.

Around Halloween, my monster began to hear from his union representative a little more often. They asked for impact statements from both of us regarding how the suspension had affected our family, finances, and mental health. We learned there would be a trial (for lack of a better word) regarding what should happen to my monster. They needed to determine if he had crossed the line or if they had made a mistake. I will admit the whole thing seemed shady, but that's only if I was getting the whole story. I wondered if his boss just hadn't liked my monster or if something a little illegal was happening on that mountain, and they didn't trust him to keep their secret. I couldn't tell.

Either way, preparation made the holidays, well, horrible. The looming dark cloud made interactions difficult with just about everyone in that small town. My monster's evil was winning, and I was losing my battle with my own demons. My depression was at a scary point; all I remember was starting to hear voices. These voices came to me in the night—in my dreams, in the shadows of my dark room when it was quiet. I felt consumed by an overwhelming desire to... die.

My monster had won. That's all I could keep telling myself. There was no happy ending for me. I wanted to go home. I wanted my mother, and I wanted to be safe. I wanted to go whatever waited for me in Heaven. I wanted to go home.

One night, my monster got exceedingly drunk. We were watching a movie, and in his drunken state, he began telling me what a whore I was. He said I was never good enough for him and that no matter what I did or how hard I worked, I could and would never satisfy him. He reminded me that any hole would do, but the frustrating part for him was that he "had to look at [my] disappointing face when [he] fucked [me]." He said I was such a turnoff, that's why he "only fucked [me] from behind."

I'd had enough.

Enough.

I grabbed a knife from the kitchen and locked myself in the bathroom with a pen and paper. I wanted to go home. I wanted away from the pain, from the mistake I made by falling in love with this wretched monster. I couldn't handle it. I slumped on the floor, an ocean of tears pouring from my eyes. I grabbed the knife and put it to my left wrist.

Lengthwise, Beth. It'll go faster.

Then I remembered I needed to say goodbye. I wanted to tell my truth because there was no way I would let him get away without someone questioning the torture he'd made me endure. Someone would have to charge him with my death, right? Maybe that was the ultimate way to make the world see what a horrific man he was.

Pen to paper, I wrote:

I'm sorry. I'm so sorry. If you all only knew this pain. If you all knew how much suffering I've endured at the hands of the man who promised to love me and take care of me. He's guilty. I swear it, he's guilty of this.

Now, to my babies... my precious babies...

I stopped. I was crying so hard the air had been stripped from my lungs. Perhaps I wouldn't need the knife after all. I already couldn't breathe; maybe my body would die of heartbreak.

My babies. My little gifts that were given to just me. I couldn't leave them, could I? Who would tell them that I abandoned them? Who would explain that their mommy wasn't strong enough to stay just for them? Who would take care of them and raise them to be the good humans I knew they would be one day?

My babies... no.

No, no, no.

I put the pen down and pushed the kitchen knife across the floor to the other side of the bathroom.

In the most raw moment of my life, I collapsed on the floor and cried until I vomited. I couldn't leave my children in the arms of that man—that monster. I had to stay; I had to protect them at all costs.

I cleaned up my mess, washed my face, crumpled up my would-be suicide note, and threw it under my sink to throw away later.

I could hear my monster snoring in the living room, passed out from too much alcohol. I placed the knife back in the block, taking a moment to promise never to go back to it. I sat on the couch, pretending to have never left. I placed my hand on my monster's knee, which woke him with a violent force.

"Are you touching me without permission, woman?!"

"I'm sorry, Sir," I whispered, chin down, eyes lowered.

"Let's go to bed. I have plans for you."

WE ANCHORED OURSELVES ONTO A CHURCH, which made us feel good. I encouraged him to stay involved with as many God-fearing men as possible, which seemed to go pretty well. I was making friends that I felt were decent enough, even though I was rotting like a six-month-old corpse on the inside. I would pray during church services for God to *intervene* at all costs. I pictured my monster going to jail so many times because he was found guilty of majorly violating someone's rights. I prayed that justice would prevail, but I hoped justice would favor the department, not my monster. I was horrible, I know. I was so remarkably desperate for peace; I wanted it at all costs.

Time marched on. Donald Trump had been elected president, much to my monster's excitement. The number of profanities he'd screamed about a woman running for president was exhausting. He would preach to our children that no woman should *ever* hold office, especially for president of the United States of America. He would say, "God didn't make women to rule. He made women to serve men and serve men alone!"

I was so ashamed to be a woman.

The holidays came and went. We smiled. Santa came to our snowy home. We had friends visit. I did what I could to keep our family afloat.

It was officially 2017. We still didn't have answers. I was due back at work after the Christmas break, and time couldn't fly by fast enough.

On my second day back, I looked at my phone and saw nine missed calls and several texts from my monster. Something was urgent. I excused myself to the restroom and called him. I just knew it was bad news.

We had an answer. He had a date and time for his determination meeting—the first of February, at the Northern Office, which was approximately a four-hour drive.

The days dripped by slower than the snow was melting outside our windows. I took the day off work and got the kids out of school. We woke up early, prepared for battle, and drove the long distance to find out my monster's fate. I watched the sunrise as the miles slipped by. Our car was silent and heavy with emotional exhaustion. When we reached our destination, my monster—in a suit, tie, and cowboy boots—looked me in the eyes and said something I'll never forget:

"I love you. Thank you for being my rock during all this."

My heart and brain were so scrambled I wasn't sure what to do. I'd spent so many hours hoping this man would get what he deserved because my body was tired, and my soul was broken. I opened my Bible and searched for answers. I helped the kids stay entertained and promised them something good to eat when we got out of there.

After about an hour and a half, my monster called me. He asked if I knew anything about another town—someplace close to where we had moved from when we owned our cookie-cutter house. Confused, I said I'd never heard of it. He simply said, "Okay, you might want to look it up. I think that's where we have to go. I'll explain more in a second when I come back to the car."

I was pissed. I'm still kind of pissed about it, even though I know why it happened.

He came back to the car and explained that the captain and other supervisors gave him two options: resign or relocate.

I can't go into further detail about this outcome other than to say the Federal Government is really good at hiding things. I am still not sure what exactly happened, but those were the choices we were given. Of course, my monster chose relocation, and he chose an area where we were still a little familiar. But it meant moving from the town I was absolutely enamored with—uprooting our children again and starting life over... again.

My ultra-planner, can-do attitude took over, knowing we wouldn't make it home if I wasn't the most positive person on the planet. I flipped off God secretly and bit my tongue until tears welled up in my fire-breathing eyes.

It shouldn't be this hard.

16

"Darling, you have outgrown the circus."

— S.C. LOURIE

PUTTING A HOUSE ON THE MARKET THAT ONLY MORONS LIKE US wanted in the first place was impossible. It was quirky, ugly, and even with the improvements we'd made on both the bathrooms, it was still something we couldn't make appealing. But we weren't wallowing in self-pity. We set our sights on the new life ahead and pushed forward.

My monster was given his gun, badge, and patrol truck back, with limited use. He wasn't allowed to do more than office work until the relocation took effect in April. Until then, I was working at the elementary school, and we were figuring out what it would take to get us out of the town we loved so much. My monster's temper was softer—no telling if it was because he was humbled or grateful. I just knew mine was on the brink of boiling over. The justice was unfair. I couldn't believe God would again punish me and our children when we were the innocent victims. But there we were.

The plan was to, once again, have my monster move ahead of us while I stayed back to clean our place enough to put it on the market. We would put it on the market when he moved; that way, the kids and I could finish the school year and move with him on the first day of summer vacation.

I was in pieces. The kids were in pieces. I could not believe this was about to be our life after everything we had suffered through to make it our own. I screamed at God so many times. I felt so abandoned. I refused to close my eyes and picture a happy life ever again. All hope in me died, and it was noticeable. Coworkers constantly asked if I was okay. I wasn't. When I spoke to family members on the phone, I spoke of peace and excitement because I could not tell the truth.

What was the truth anymore?

April 1 came around, and my monster headed south to report to his new station. My father and his wife lent my monster their incredibly nice trailer for him to park at the barracks so he didn't have to pay money to live onsite where he was located. The good news was he didn't have cell service there. I wouldn't be harassed all the time when he was there, and I wouldn't have to talk to him at all hours of the night. There was a landline that he was allowed to use once a day, but that was an insignificant amount of time to me.

I busied myself with all the work I had to do. I was angry but pretty free to make a lot of my own choices. He was over nine hours away, so I wasn't afraid or looking over my shoulder. In fact, the distance seemed to have made us… *distant*. I wasn't sure what was happening, but we rarely fought on the phone. I no longer cared about his threats, and he knew he was powerless to follow through with them anyway, so I suppose we concluded that there was no need. The children didn't miss him at all, either. Sure, there was stress living on that big mountain all alone, in a house that was barely livable, much less sellable.

However, the three of us bonded like never before. I let them sleep in bed with me on weekends, they had friends over, and we went to school and town functions together. Were we struggling financially? Sure! But that wasn't new. We weren't walking on eggshells. That's all that mattered.

At one point, I was talking to my monster on his landline and heard a knock on his trailer door. He scrambled, uncharacteristically nervous. The loud crack of the RV door came through the phone. I heard giggling female voices. Then things got muffled a bit, and all I could make out were whispers.

Keep in mind, he was at an isolated location at an off-season fire station. No one else should have been there, save for the occasional janitor or firefighter chief coming in to check on equipment.

My naïve brain finally realized what was happening: an almost audible lightbulb turning on and bursting above my head.

He was cheating on me.

I hung up, turned my phone off, and screamed into my pillow at the top of my lungs.

After *everything* he had put me through, after *everything* I had changed and was changing for this man, he had women with him. The fire burning in my belly, the rage I had coursing through my bones; I had never been so angry in all my life. Was I mad at him? Absolutely. But the fury set ablaze within was directed at one person: ME.

I had waited. I had forgiven. I had pushed through the bad and did all I could to focus on the beautiful. I stayed for my children—the children who were happier without their daddy being home. What a fool. What an absolute FOOL I was. How could I have believed this would go any other way?

I took off my wedding rings and began looking for ways to stay in our little town, just the kids and me. Could the three of us live off my small wages at the school and be okay? There were apartments nearby—could I do it? I went to work without my wedding rings. My choice was justified, and I wanted no reminders of him. He messed up *big time*. And I knew he knew it. There was no lie that he could come up with that would make any of this go away. I had an out, and this time—*Biblically* (according to my monster)—I was allowed to leave.

However, you and I can clearly see this isn't where my story ends. Still holding a bunch of unread pages in your hand, right?

If you are disappointed in me, I get it. I would love to tell you I deserve it. I would love to say that it would have been incredibly easy for me to abandon everything and run. The problem is I was still a victim of abuse.

When I turned my phone back on (a whole 24 hours later), I had a lot of new voicemails. They were filled with apologies and anger, and then more apologies laced with fervent threats.

Sitting in my car in the school's parking lot, I called him back on my lunch break. He was pretty broken, and I spewed rage from all my pores. I wondered if this was how it felt to be him— to be that angry. The difference was I had a legitimate reason to *be* angry. I told him that I drew the line when it came to cheating (I mean, duh… right?) and that I wanted to stay in our town.

He told me he wasn't cheating on me and that they were just two women (he specified that they were ugly women because that made things better) staying at the barracks and needed to use the phone. Without a doubt, I did not believe him. I muted my phone while he talked, begging for affirmation that I believed him. I screamed at God:

THIS NEEDS TO END! DON'T YOU CARE ABOUT ME AT ALL?! WHAT THE HELL DID I DO TO MAKE YOU SO DAMN ANGRY AT ME? I'M A GOOD PERSON, FATHER. A GOOD FREAKING PERSON!!

"Hello? Did I lose you? Where are you?"

"I'm here."

"You're here, wha—"

"Yeah, I am no longer calling you 'Sir'. Don't you dare tell me to because, time and time again, you prove that you are not the type of person who can handle a title like that. The bedroom was the only place that was ever supposed to stay. And I am absolutely done with all that, too. I am here at work; I know you were with at least one of those women, so I am staying here, and we can figure out how life will work later."

I hung up the phone. My heart was in my throat and beating so loudly in my ears I was pretty sure the noise could be heard by the parents I greeted as I walked back onto campus. I was brazened, in control, and more than anything, I knew even he couldn't argue with my reasonings. Where was this strength coming from, though? Like, WHAT? I walked into the first-grade classroom I spent my days in and was beaming. The teacher asked if I'd had a good lunch. I winked and smiled. Had David beaten Goliath? I was on top of the world.

He might have been abusive, but his emotions were always at the forefront of each move he made. It's probably why he wasn't a good cop and why he wasn't able to connect with others socially. He called back again and again. I wasn't fooled, but I was willing to listen.

A couple of weeks went by with a lot of back and forth between us. We talked a lot, probably more than when we went to counseling after he was arrested. I was no longer calling him "Sir," and though it was awkward for a little while, I was free from a term that embarrassed me in public and shamed me in private.

The biggest argument I had that helped me win the luxury was that the children were scolding me for not calling him "Sir." I could tell it ignited his internal fury. I felt like Dobby when he got Harry Potter's sock. I was beyond free, not only because he wasn't around, but some inner force had also taken hold of me —almost training me for what was ahead. I did all I could to sell the house and spend time with friends before the end of the school year. But before I knew it, it was May. Mother's Day, to be exact.

My monster made plans to come back home to pick up the kids and me, just to turn around and go to the new town we would live in. He wanted to look at houses with us and even took me to the zoo to see all the new enclosures they had built. Fun fact about Bethany? She hates zoos. So, that should say a little bit about the man I was married to. Did he know me at all?

It was a long weekend, but I tried to enjoy it. My monster was soft-hearted, not raising his voice once during the three days. I was suspicious as crap; wouldn't you be? He held my hand; he instructed our children to be extra nice to me. He listened to my ideas on which houses I liked. The kids and I loathed the town. Nothing would have been a good fit, though. Not even Oz itself. The three of us wanted to be back where we were. We wanted to stay where we felt rooted, amongst the trees and clean air. But as had become the routine, life had different plans.

We arrived at our house late Sunday night. He was to sleep and turn right around to go back to his trailer early Monday morning. I couldn't wait for him to leave, but at the same time, the tiniest beacon of hope was suddenly lit. Maybe he was actually happy. Maybe the chaos we had endured the previous year had taken its toll on him. Maybe this opportunity, where he was isolated day in and day out, over nine hours away from his family with no real way to communicate other than one phone call a day, made him see his priorities clearly for the first time. Maybe, just maybe, things were going to be better.

May flew by. I was prioritizing and prepping for our move.

We'd found a tiny rental with no kitchen cabinets but a lot of space. The landlord said we could have goats and chickens—two consolation prizes I wasn't sad about. And I suppose another great thing was that the government was paying movers for us; I only had to pack boxes if I wanted to. My monster planned to return for the final moving day so that the four of us could travel the nine hours together. He surprised me by returning a week early, though—showing up at my school with roses, asking my boss to let me go home early.

Okay, God... I see You. Am I supposed to trust this now? Are You trying to make up for all the times You allowed him to torment me? Please, please give me the strength to trust him. Please.

The last day of school still hurts me to this day. When I think about the tears, broken hearts, goodbyes... my chest hurts. There are a few pictures I look at from time to time: ones taken by parents of me hugging and crying with their students. One kid, *my* student to whom I was his 1:1 aide... yeah. Those are heart-wrenching pictures. The two of us sobbed because we had to leave one another. I loved that child and the bond I had created with them. I loved that area and the community I had sunken into. I loved walking through the historic area that dated back well before the 1840s and saying hello to the people I knew on the street. I miss it so badly, even now.

The movers were there, loading up their truck. We had neighbors and friends come by to wish us farewell. The day took longer than expected, so we were in for a long drive to our new house.

It was time, though. It was time to say goodbye to yet another pain-filled, yucky chapter in our lives. The only one who was happy was the one who had gotten us into this mess in the first place. Just before we left the town line, that monster of mine got pulled over. The cop had no probable cause, no reason for the stop. I watched from my rearview mirror with a small smile on my face. Maybe this was what I needed to see. Maybe this moment was a gift. It wasn't that the town was corrupt; it wasn't that the town didn't like us as a family.

Maybe the town just didn't like *him*.

Maybe, just maybe, I was the only one dumb enough to think anyone did.

17

"When you are born in a burning house, you think the whole world is on fire. But it's not."

— RICHARD KADREY

ISOLATION IS FUNNY. SOMETIMES, IT TAKES A GREAT DEAL OF effort to realize how truly far away you are from the rest of the world, especially when you are used to it—to the silence, to the long drives, to the idea that you are a forgotten piece of history because no one ever visits you. But after living high up in the mountains of a pretty isolated area, I learned that community was what you made of it.

No, the shopping centers filled with Target, Hobby Lobby, or Five Below aren't within a five-minute drive. No, you can't find competing Starbucks stores on each corner. Instead, you have Wednesday night soccer games with the same groups of people, the same teams, the same referees... all of whom you'll see on Friday night for the Farmer's Market and live music. I loved that about where we were.

This new town was far from the romantic, old-town feel I'd

fallen in love with. Oh, it was old town all right, but these folks were not friendly to new faces. They most especially were not friendly to the family of the new law enforcement officer in town, and I absolutely could not understand why. I don't think it had anything to do with his badge or even his department. I spent a lot of my time unpacking boxes, wondering if he had already developed a reputation I was unaware of. Either way, this town was not in a hurry to get to know us.

We had no trees, no river, and no mountains. We *did* have a beautiful view *of* mountains off our back porch that overlooked a large yard with lush green grass, which was this place's only redeeming quality. The landlords were overbearing and made me incredibly uncomfortable. They had a "we can drop in whenever" attitude, and I hated it.

Admittedly, I struggled. I struggled immensely. I did not want to adjust, and I did not want to acknowledge that my unhappiness was consuming me. I wasn't calling my friends or my family anymore. The more I didn't call, the more I realized they didn't call either. I constantly suspected (hoped?) that my monster was cheating on me. I was definitely not someone anyone wanted to be around.

I worked on the house to make it feel like home, though I knew I had left my heart 455+ miles away in the deep mountains in the north.

I did not enroll the children in any events that summer. We were close enough (about two hours) to my father that we spent time at his place and his neighbor's pool. My grandmother had moved in with him, too. She was approaching her 90th birthday, so I spent as much time with her as I could. She... my goodness. She was my best friend. She was the only one in the family who never questioned me. I could write an entire book on my relationship with her, and perhaps I shall. My Nana, my gift, my world... she was getting up there in age, and despite my father's efforts to make it seem like she'd live forever, the truth was, my precious Nana was in his house on hospice.

Time was short.

My monster was off on assignment after assignment. I was thankful not to have to ask permission to go to my father's house. I simply had to communicate that I was going. He knew my love for Nana, and in fact, he loved her, too. If I'm completely transparent, I was often jealous of how he looked at and treated her. I had great hopes that when I was an old woman, I'd finally be adored the way he did her.

On the long car rides, I'd talk to God or whoever was up there (remember how angry I was), admitting a few things to be clear-minded in my depression.

So... I'm here because of her. You knew I wouldn't have been able to see her. You knew my life would never be the same if I couldn't bring her these special cupcakes that my mother used to make just for her on her 90th birthday. You knew I would not have made it. You knew I wasn't strong enough. Okay. I get it. Thank You. Thank You for giving me this opportunity. But before You plan to take her from me, please... grant me the ability to love on her. Let me hold her hand. Please give me the chance, hours of chances, to make her smile and remind her that she made me who I am. That my childhood would never have been magic. That I wouldn't know what it is to be a fierce woman without her. Please. I swear, my heart cannot break one more time. Do not rob me of the ability to say goodbye.

For a full month straight, I said words like this on each car ride. I spent as many days with her as I could. I gave her those cupcakes on her birthday, which was the last cognizant set of conversations I had with her. In August, I was driving home from some errand and noticed the sun setting behind a few wispy clouds. The hues of orange and auburn were astounding, but the one thing that caught my eye more than anything was the way the light was beaming upward: almost like a direct spotlight on Heaven. My soul knew.

The following day, our precious family dog passed away suddenly. Roscoe was my boy, the first baby my monster and I had. He was 15, and for a large Australian Shepherd, that was an incredible age. Our family grieved, screaming, crying, helping him to his final resting place. Thankfully, my monster was home and could help bury and say goodbye to our "Boofy Boy." I was holding our oldest, who had bonded so deeply with Roscoe—the two were inseparable—when my phone rang.

"Sis, it's Dad. It's your Nana, honey. We don't have much time."

We dropped our shovels, grabbed bags of overnight clothes, and ran to the car. My monster was nice when it came to death, but only in the way a mortician could be. He had seen so much death—especially regarding animals—that he almost had no sympathy for it. And with what I had experienced when my mother died, I couldn't help but put my wall up. I was in no position to deal with crass, emotionless conversation. This time, though, on this car ride, he was silent. I was thankful for that.

My father's house was filled with family who had driven from all over the state. My Nana was the matriarch, even though she was an identical twin. Her sister lived a good distance away and was in no condition to be there (twins are like that, but *these* two were *very* like that). The energy of the house was a mix of deeply cut wounds and soft-hearted joy. Nana had touched more lives than we could count, but it wasn't time to think about that. It was our time to show her the three generations under one roof who owed everything to her.

I was on the brink of collapse as I went through the hallway to her room. She always said I had a sad heart but wore it beautifully on my sleeve so that others didn't have to be ashamed of theirs. I wanted to throw mine in the river or back at God because I'd never asked for such a thing. She said I had the soul of a poet, and one day she'd hoped to hold my writing in her hands. I'd failed her. Goddamn it, she didn't know me at all! I'd kept so many secrets in those 12 years, so many things I couldn't be brave enough to tell her. I knew what she'd say. But none of that mattered now.

The door was slightly open, just enough to see my uncle, Nana's youngest son. He was there, holding it in as best he could. I pushed open the door with trembling hands. My eyes made their way to her bed. She was just... there. Her eyes were closed, and her chest moved so slowly, up and then down—my Nana.

When I was a child, she *loved* to nap. I hated that time of day because, after all, she was there to visit! Who sleeps while they're on vacation, especially when they're visiting their grand-kids?! But I remember vividly that I never wanted to see her sleeping. Even when I was four, I was afraid that if I ever saw her sleeping, she wouldn't wake up. Do you think it's true that some of our quirky fears as children wind up being an odd foreshadowing of something when you're an adult?

I think of that all too often.

I sat in the chair beside her bed. I grabbed her hand and laid my head on her chest; her gargling, wheezing breaths were like daggers straight into my heart.

"Nana, what's going on? You just had to bring the whole family down here because you needed attention, didn't you?" A failed attempt to solidify our sarcastic, feisty bond fell flat in the room that betrayed my hope. I couldn't bear it. I just couldn't bear it.

My children came in. I didn't force them to stay long because I don't care how close you are with a person, at ages ten and eight, they didn't need to endure that kind of discomfort. My monster came in. "Thank you for all the laughs. I hope you're at peace."

I could have She-Hulked him into the next century.

The night went on; she stayed the same—breathing, but not with us. At about one o'clock in the morning, most of us went to bed with the promise to take turns watching over her. About four o'clock, my father entered the room where we were sleeping.

"Sis, this might be it. Come on, come be with your Nana."

My father. He and I didn't have the best relationship, as I've stated before. But we agreed that his mother was genuinely the most iconic example of what second chances can look like. My father and his two brothers grew up with a very different version of the woman I knew and loved. She was a raging alcoholic, which ultimately cost her full custody of her three boys, back in the late 1960s. Imagine that—not only a divorced woman during that period, but a woman the courts deemed unworthy of raising her children? She went on to be one of the first women in Alcoholics Anonymous, sponsoring a few hundred women in her time. As I later found out, she saved many lives. Just before her 90th birthday, she was awarded her 50th sobriety chip. So few in recovery achieve such things; I was in awe.

I walked with my father over to Nana's room. This time, her breathing was much worse. I asked for a moment alone with her.

I felt awkward, like I was supposed to do or say something profound. That's what Nana would do, anyway. I held her hand and took a picture. Her hand in mine, so frail. I was enamored with how much her hands had done, had seen. I wondered if she liked her hands or if she had a complex about them. Her wedding ring shone in the dim light. She'd remarried the absolute love of her life when I was about two years old. Good ol' Grandpa Fat Jack, as I called him.

He was a WWII gunner, and he did *not* talk about it. He loved my Nana like no other, but you wouldn't know. He was so grumpy, so fierce. But when Nana walked into a room, his eyes twinkled. Grandpa Jack had a stroke when I was in high school. That stroke changed him into the goofiest, loving man. It drove Nana crazy! He'd smack her on the rear end when she'd walk by. I can still hear her say, "Jaaaack! Stop that!" and he'd giggle with his limited speech. When Grandpa Jack died, I thought I was going to lose Nana, too. But she trucked on, brokenhearted but filled with love for him.

That was it.

"Nana," I whispered, with my head on her chest. "You know what? I know you're being stubborn. You gave me that gift, and I'm thankful for it. But it's okay to go now. It really is. And you know what I just realized? Grandpa Jack is probably getting annoyed waiting on your behind."

At the mention of his name, her eyebrows went up. She hadn't moved an inch in days. But saying his name, it was as if I spoke magic.

Holding back gallons of tears, I said, "Don't you want to go see him? Hmm? Grandpa Jack is waiting for you. Don't make him grumpy in Heaven... that'll just make things awkward."

"Hmmmmmm," Nana hummed. She took a deep breath, and she looked lighter. Happier. I was bawling. I told her I loved her and would miss her every day for the rest of my life. I thanked her for being my best friend.

An additional 12 hours went by with no change. My monster had to return to work that next day, so we needed to leave. We said our goodbyes one more time, promising to come back if things changed.

We passed my eldest uncle on the road on the way back home.

He was with her for one hour, her final missing piece, and she took her last breath.

I hadn't even gotten home yet. I couldn't comprehend a world without her. I couldn't grasp the fact that I would never know her secrets, her magic, her ability to grab her crappy life by the horns and take charge. I had lost my best friend.

My monster jetted off to work the next day.

Two days later, my precious children had their first day at their new school.

Life had to resume.

I had to resume.

Again.

It shouldn't have to be this hard.

18

"You are so brave and quiet I forget you are suffering."

— ERNEST HEMINGWAY

NEW TOWN, NEW SCHOOL, NEW HEARTACHE? NO PROBLEM!

We were there to take each day in stride, and boy, if I didn't make sure we did just that. A huge fire broke out at the end of August that my monster had to investigate. He was on camera for many local news stations as he looked into how the fire started. The kids and I were excited to see him, so we saved the clip on our DVR. We showed him the news clip when he returned home a few days later.

He became enraged.

He had gained some weight over the last couple of years, and seeing firsthand what he looked like made him furious. He announced he was done drinking and wanted to get on the Ketogenic diet and join Brazilian Jiu-Jitsu (BJJ).

Um. Okay.

Wait, that's all it took to get him to stop drinking? *THAT*? Not the getting-arrested-for-hurting-your-wife part?

Whatever.

We were embarking on yet *another* way to live, but this time, the children would be like their daddy and join BJJ, training and making themselves better, stronger people. How on earth could I argue?

To my dismay, he offered to allow me to join, too. But I wasn't allowed to train with men, and there weren't any women's—only classes. Women in BJJ aren't all that common. I decided it wasn't my thing but I was there for support. A decision I would come to regret in about a year.

The training gym we joined was filled with a completely different group of people than I had ever encountered. As a kid, I played softball, so I was familiar with sports people. But these humans? Man, were they ever intense... and attractive! They all had the most in-shape bodies with the most genuinely kind spirits. They wanted you to succeed; they wanted your kids to succeed. Heck—they'd be thrilled to watch your goldfish succeed. I wasn't great with fitting in because I was always a spectator, never a participant, but I was still greeted each time I walked in. I got asked week after week when I was going to join. I never had the desire because I knew what the fights would be like at home.

The gym was a 45-minute drive one way, and my monster had all of us going a minimum of three times per week. I had to go because his session began after our children's session, so *someone* had to stay and watch the kids. This meant that for at least three nights a week, I was in the car for an hour and a half and sitting at the gym for at least two and a half hours. I felt like a total fool, but my monster was *happy*. His anger was not often targeted at me; he was no longer drinking, and he was putting his mental and physical health first. We even reconnected with his brother and his brother's family. I began to want to be involved with life again.

It wasn't complete paradise. Don't get me wrong, we were still arguing. I was less meek, though, since I no longer had to call him "Sir," but I was constantly threatened with what he "could" do. Every time he would disagree with something, I'd be the problem. Each time he was upset about work or being unable to train, I would bear the brunt. I tried to keep the peace, which was poisoning my soul.

The more he trained, the more arrogant he became. It was astonishing—like watching a car accident, incapable of helping or turning away. He made other people uncomfortable.

Everything came down to Jiu-Jitsu. Everything. Even after his first tournament was a complete disaster, he trained harder. He started training when he was out on assignments. It was all-consuming. He lost so much weight he started giving me subtle hints that I should work out, too. We ran together a few times, training for a 5K that supported law enforcement and their families. Eventually, he told me I should exercise more because he wasn't finding me attractive.

"It's a wife's job to turn her man on," he'd say.

I felt like scum. My weight was always an issue for me, but he had never made me feel ashamed for it (for other things, yes, but he was pretty sensitive about this). He finally crossed that line, so I asked if I could join a gym. I would do a morning workout after I took the kids to school, and then I would do one at a different gym while they were at training and would come back before his training started.

He required a few things:

1. I had to research which gym would work, and then he would have to visit for approval.
2. Once a gym was chosen, I was to take a picture of my outfit before I left the house and text him with it

when I was going. I could not drive away without his approval of my outfit.

3. Once I arrived at the gym, I had to let him know by sending *another* picture in the gym bathroom mirror to prove I was there.

4. When my workout was complete, I had to send him one last picture in the gym bathroom mirror to prove I was still wearing the permitted outfit, and I needed to make sure I looked like I'd sweated in it.

5. Finally, I was required to text him when I got home.

This was every single day.

There was a day when I missed one of those steps, and he screamed at me for two days straight. He accused me of cheating and said I couldn't be trusted. I wasn't allowed to return to the gym until he cooled off.

I loathed hearing about Jiu-Jitsu. I got to the point where I hated being in the training gym, sitting on the bench that pretty much had my name on it permanently. I'd read and finished several books from that bench. I was over it. But I could not deny the distance it created between my monster and me. When he was on the road, he spent more time training or looking for places to train. I was hitting my own gym seven times a week, and I wasn't hating what that dedication was doing for my body. The children loved the training and the peace in the house, too, so how could I deny them the opportunity to do something they enjoyed?

Christmas came and went, but there was a stirring—an uneasy feeling developing within me. I was disconnected from my monster, though we laid next to each other each night. I have almost no memory of how or even if he reacted. I just knew that New Year's Eve arrived. I was feeling apathetic, at best. Midnight struck, and I went to sleep.

When I woke up, it was January 1, 2018, and I was no longer the same Bethany.

———

YES, we are back to the beginning, where this book started. You've stayed with me all this time, getting the full-spectrum background of how life came to be for me in 2018. Was it the worst abuse you've ever heard of? Maybe for some of you, but maybe not for others. I suppose each human has their own threshold of what they can and cannot handle. Whatever your brink is, you're allowed; what isn't allowed is someone crossing it.

How are you, by the way? Are you okay? I'd be lying if I said I didn't worry about the wonderful humans who picked this book up and have read it this far. I hope you're taking care of yourself. I hope you are safe, that you are loved, and that you know your worth.

We'll come back to that in a little while.

———

NOT MANY SIGNIFICANT things happened in the first half of 2018. Our oldest hit four years of being seizure-free, and our youngest began their love for video game design. We had a new puppy who came at the exact right time. She was (and still is!) my whole world. Everything seemed to be blasé and routine.

We joined a church that seemed okay. The congregation and staff loved all first responders and military members, so my husband was worshipped whenever he attended. I had no friends whatsoever, but I stayed focused on the gym and doing as much as I could with my babies. They turned eleven and nine that year, and the realization that my time with them was dwin-dling was beginning to tap into my brain.

We did a lot of family trips to the lake, the river, and even went to a theme park. I was spoken to like I was trash almost constantly, being reminded that even though he was tired from training, he could always punish me anytime he wished. I questioned everything, and that didn't feel good.

During the end of summer break, our children had the opportunity to go to a week-long church camp. I had never been without them for that long, but I knew this would be good for them. They were growing up, after all; I had to let them learn to fly a bit without me.

I had not spent a week with my monster, just the two of us, since before our oldest was born. At that point, it had been over 11 years: 11 years of chaos, hurt, distrust, and abuse. Remember, I had already decided that I was going to leave my monster and was searching for the exact time. Was my heart excited about the week we were about to spend together? No. Was I heartbroken when he informed me he was still going to work that week because he "had to?" Also, no. I just knew I couldn't wait for the children to come back home... and they hadn't even left yet.

I packed their clothes and supplies and stuffed their back-packs and Bibles with secret notes to remind them I loved and believed in them. We took them to the church and left them in the hands of a bunch of people we barely knew. We got in the car and just... what? What were we supposed to do?

As it turns out, we went on a few dates that week: an escape room, dinner, the movies, and the river. Honestly, I only remember the escape room and a little blurb from a restaurant we went to. Ten minutes ago, I went into an old Instagram account to double-check the facts. I'd long forgotten the rest. What I do remember from that week was the fact that I had a ruptured blood vessel in my right eye. No one—not a church member, not a stranger, not the waitress at the restaurant—said a thing to me. No one questioned it; no one voiced concern. Not a thing. But in every picture I just saw, it is *obvious*. I can't believe I'd forgotten about it.

Had my monster caused my eye to look like that? I don't know. I know he hadn't hit me. But the fact remains that I don't remember. It might have happened during sex, as the force and aggressiveness in that department were not off the table, so walking away with measurable injuries or welts I hadn't agreed to or remembered receiving was not uncommon.

Fun fact: I don't often get upset when I think about all the people who later said things like, "I thought there might have been something going on, but I didn't want to be rude and ask," but sitting with these pictures right now, at this moment, I feel betrayed. And that happens. The trauma wounds of a survivor do not always stem from their abuser. The humans they lost trust in throughout that period often bring about the most hurt when the survivors' memories surface. But listen, my friends—when those emotions bubble back up, it's important to soothe them with whatever tools are rolling around in your emotional toolbox and find a place to forgive them. It's going to suck. And it's okay.

"*What was our relationship like at that point?*" you ask? "*Was he still verbally, mentally, and emotionally abusive to you?*" Yes. Yes, he was. Anytime we argued, he'd be insatiably passive-aggressive, reminding me that he had unyielding power but couldn't use it in case I wanted to call the cops again. He constantly reminded me that I took a picture with a man at a conference. He told me all the time when he was angry that I was a waste of space and that I only ever belonged on my knees in front of him. Anytime —and I mean anytime—my monster was angry, it was my fault.

I began to keep the voicemails he'd leave me of all the horrible things he'd say when I missed his call.

My feet were still very much walking on eggshells. The difference was that my calluses were thick, and my heart had no fight.

19

"Alone and damaged is better than lifeless with you."

— PERRY POETRY

IT WAS LATE SEPTEMBER, AND MY MONSTER WAS ON HIS WAY HOME from an assignment in another state. His absence that summer was rigorous, spanning three weeks at a time, with only a few days at home before another three-week tour. Between fire season and marijuana eradication, he was busy. While he was gone that time, I finally cracked. The same something within me screamed violently to leave him—as it did each time I'd lie in our bed alone.

The voice was always a nagging but deafening plea to grab our children, escape to the end of the universe, and not look back; the difference this time was that I listened to it. I'd heard that still, small voice echoing that the time had come. I finally mustered the courage and decided that I'd had enough. It must have shown, too, because my monster was angry... really angry. His threatening text messages increased each minute I decisively delayed my responses. When I wouldn't apologize for not answering his call or for making the excuse that I was speaking to a long-winded family member (which wasn't a lie), his accusations of infidelity and threats of being majorly punished grew exponentially.

There was a point where he'd tried to call me, but I was asleep and did not answer. When I awoke the next morning, I texted an apology, letting him know what had happened.

"It's okay. I took care of the problem myself," his text said.

Meaning, he wanted me to "assist" him in his "need," but since I didn't, he rubbed one out all on his own. He told me I would be punished for that. Funny, he only threatened sexual punishments when feeling out of control. And trust me, he was.

Another night was gone, and he was another day closer to being home. I woke to another text, but only one this time.

"I don't love you anymore."

My out.

My release.

The text message I'd been waiting on for 13 1/2 years.

In his anger the night before, he'd sent me a host of messages that proved to me that he was back to drinking, and I knew that if I were home when he arrived, I'd be in immediate danger. Waking up to that message filled me with peace that I couldn't explain but also with fear that I now *had* to explain.

The time had come.

Truth.

I called my father and released over a decade's worth of truths I no longer had to hide. My monster would be home that evening... my father demanded that I take my children and my dog and get to safety. Though I didn't have the greatest relationship with my father, I ran to him faster than I knew I could. My children only knew we were staying at Grandpa's for the weekend. I knew that our lives were about to change forever.

I told my father and stepmother everything. *EVERYTHING*. I

explained how I was in a marriage where I was a slave to my husband. Where I was required to call him "Sir" at all times and was punished sexually if I did anything wrong. I told them how my husband did not consider unwanted sexual advances "rape" because we were married and sex within marriage was a God-given right for men. I told them that I wasn't allowed to hang out with friends and was most certainly not allowed to go anywhere without his permission. I showed them all the pictures I'd taken of myself when I arrived at the gym and just before leaving to prove I was wearing clothes he approved of. I went into further detail about the time he was arrested for knocking me unconscious and ultimately trying to squeeze the air from my lungs in a drunken rage over our oldest child's brain surgery being scheduled. How I lied to the District Attorney, saying that the arresting officers that night were stretching the truth to meet a quota so that my monster didn't lose his job. I explained why I stayed: if he lost his job, we'd lose our health insurance, meaning our child couldn't have their life-saving surgeries.

My father cried. He was furious. My stepmother lovingly cradled me and affirmed that I could stay with them as long as needed.

I called my sibling. I spoke my truth. I've never heard them so violently quiet. They truly had never liked my monster, as I'd thought, but loved me enough to endure him. The guilt set in for my precious sibling, and they apologized more times than I could count. Each time, their anger grew louder. I couldn't tell if they were mad at my husband or me. At that moment, I didn't blame them if they were angry at both. I know I was.

By sunset that night, my phone was blowing up with messages from my very desperate monster. He teeter-tottered between realizing the error of his ways and being spit-fire fuming at me for not answering him. He'd say things like: "I just need my wife," "I miss you so badly, but I didn't know the right way to say it," and, "I messed up and won't do it again." But then, he'd sprinkle those messages with, "How dare you leave me alone!" and, "You better be at the house when I get there, or else you'll be in a world of hurt."

I did not respond to him for hours. When I finally did, I spoke out against his behavior. I told him how I hated being used as his slave, how I was tired of being treated as though I was nothing, and that I was no longer interested in the emotional/mental abuse. I did not want to suffer at the hands of my vows. I did not sign up for this.

I wasn't backing down.

I told him how our youngest child physically shivered at the thought of their father returning. When I asked them about it, they said, "I just don't want him to come home. Things are better when he's not here."

That sent him over the edge. The barrage of messages, filled to the brim with brutal accusations and the fiercest gaslighting one has ever seen, came at me like a full-fledged airstrike.

I did not waver.

I looked into the eyes of my children, incapable of imagining a world where they grew up to be like their own misogynistic, homophobic, racist, angry, abusive father. I had to get out to save them. To save their future spouses. To save their dreams. It was up to me. I had to be strong.

The problem was that I couldn't stay at my father's house forever. The kids had school on Monday, and my oldest had a big cross-country race on Wednesday. Somehow, I had to go home. Somehow, I had to stick up for myself. He would get angry enough to leave... right?

Against my father's wishes, I loaded my car with the kids and our beloved dog. It was a weekend of calm before the storm, complete with a birthday cake my children made me; that's right, it'd been my birthday the week or so before. The picture my father took of me blowing out my candles still haunts me. There I was, without makeup and practically soulless, holding my babies, trying to smile. They had no idea what was coming, what was waiting for us when we got home. Nor did I. But as I pulled out of the driveway, my stepmother gave me a reassuring look that filled my belly with fire.

I can do this.

That two-hour drive back to hell was a long one, filled with every possible scenario and rehearsed lines. I only began to shake as I headed up into the foothills. I hated where we lived. He knew how to keep me as isolated as possible and did so with panache and vigor. I spotted his patrol truck in our driveway from the road. If I could see that, it meant he could see me. There was no turning back.

The kids were excited to see him. He showered me with awkward hugs and even a gift with a card I never read. We sent the children inside to get started on their bedtime routine.

"Daddy will be in in a second; I just need to talk to Mommy."

I always hated how he spoke in the third person to them. It was the little things... the proof of his disconnect was blinding.

I'd be lying if I said I was nervous. I wasn't. Not for the first time since I met him. I stood there and let him talk, apologizing for how he'd spoken to me. I didn't say a word. He hugged me again, but I didn't hug back. The phoenix within me was rising; I no longer belonged to this man.

I felt nothing.

Once the kids were asleep, safe from any displeasing and chaotic banter that was certain to follow, we sat on the couch and talked. Correction: *he* talked. At first, the apologies and requests for understanding came. It was the usual runaround I had memorized at this point. He was sorry for being so grumpy, he'd been sleeping on the ground in a tent for weeks, the people around him were mean to him, he missed me so much, blah, blah, blah.

I didn't budge.

I didn't blink.

I didn't give in.

It aggravated him, and his emotions escalated.

The blame began: I wasn't answering the phone, I wasn't calling him *Sir* like I was required to, and worst of all, how could I tell him what I told him about our child?

I let him speak until he was exhausted. My facial expression never changed. Finally, he screamed with tears bursting from his eyes like an anime character under duress, "PLEASE! TALK TO ME!"

"I have nothing to say," I whispered.

"Do you want a divorce? TELL ME YOU WANT A DIVORCE!" He was on his knees, clambering to hold me.

"I don't know."

Panic of the highest caliber cascaded across his forehead.

He held me... sobbing, begging... it was almost embarrassing.

Ultimately, we went to bed. I had an appointment in the morning to get tattoos to represent my children. I'd had the appointment set for months. It took me a long time to get my husband's approval, and since I'd already been permitted to pay for them, I wasn't missing out. Besides, I'd be away from him for the day. It was a win-win.

I laid in our California King-sized bed, begging God that the horrible man next to me wouldn't inch a millimeter closer. I would have rather been lying next to a decaying corpse. How could I have ever been married to him? How was I so brain-washed into thinking the way I was being treated was love? How had I lost myself to his delusions? Had anyone *ever* loved me the way I feel love?

There were too many questions, and sleep never came to me. I hushed my alarm before it woke the house and tip-toed into our children's rooms to quietly get them ready for school. My already-dressed monster greeted me in the kitchen, who—without so much as a "good morning"—announced that we would be driving the kids to school together because he would be escorting me to my tattoo appointment.

Complete and utter dread filled my lungs and weakened my shoulders. I know he noticed; his smirk was all too familiar.

The drive to my friend's tattoo shop was quiet at first. He forced me to hold his hand, clasping it like a child trying to keep a firm grip on their balloon in the middle of gale-force winds. We listened to music I meticulously chose to keep me secure in my new mindset. Eventually, he turned the volume of my sanity down and questioned everything we'd already discussed. He was vile, screaming obscenities and insults as though they were offerings to the gods. I'd been his willing sacrifice for 13 1/2 years, but my clear change in course direction left him baffled and fuming.

Again, I did not argue much because I discovered not doing so made him all the more frustrated. Eventually, he pulled the car over on an older, less frequently traveled road and told me to get out. For the first time in over a decade, I uttered the most powerful word I had in my arsenal: a forbidden word—a word so ghastly and disrespectful, it resulted in physical, sexual punishment anytime I dared say it:

"No."

His eyes lit up like firecrackers, catching everything within a five-mile radius ablaze.

But he did not strike. He did not even lay a finger on me. Instead, *he* got out of the car, slamming the door and screaming about calling an Uber.

Nothing motivated that man more than money. A lot of what

pissed him off deep down was that money did not impress nor matter to me. He often accused me of being money-hungry, which always made me giggle because those accusations proved how little he knew me. But because money ruled him, I knew an Uber was out of the question, and missing my tattoo appointment wouldn't happen because that would mean he'd lose out on money already spent.

So, I waited.

Of *course,* he got back in the car, and of course, he screamed at me for the next 45 minutes about what a selfish whore I was. I didn't care; I just wanted to feel some physical pain of my choosing, to remember that the best things I got from that monster beside me were my children.

He watched me like a hawk while my sweet friend and tattoo artist, Cat, prepped her eager canvas. Cat was going through the typical motions of conversation—asking how we were, how the babies were, and delighting in hearing all the details of our move back to the valley. She knew how important these tattoos were to me, as she'd watched our journey the previous few years. My monster sat oddly close and held my hand as I endured the pain. It was so uncomfortably fake.

When other artists came to see what Cat was up to, they didn't stay long; the tension in her booth was thick and off-putting. At one point, my monster wanted to get some snacks and cash for Cat's tip. The moment the shop's door shut behind him, Cat rolled me over and was like, "Babe... what's going on? Are you okay?" I only *slightly* lied because I said things weren't happy, but I was fine.

I suppose, in a way, I *was* just fine! I had an out. His text message was the final nail in the coffin that was our doomed marriage, and I was going to hold onto it until I could genuinely use it. But Cat didn't need all of that information at the time.

Besides, by the time I'd gotten up the courage to tell her I wasn't safe, he'd returned.

Such a typical movie moment, right?

After the tattoo appointment and another lengthy scream-fest about how I was a money-hungry, ungrateful bitch, I thought I might be free. He dropped me off at the house and drove away. But before I could make it across the living room, he was back inside screaming that we would pick up our children together from the bus stop and go out as a *family* to get groceries and dinner.

He wouldn't let go of my hand. I wasn't allowed out of his sight—not even to walk with the children across the store. He gripped my wrist as though he were clamoring to not fall off a cliff to his death. I played the dutiful wife in public to save face for my children. I was good, too. If I were an actress, I would have taken home every award—my name being thought of highly amongst the other EGOT winners. But this wasn't Holly-wood... and I was finally terrified.

The car ride home set into motion what would be the rest of our lives... or the end of mine.

My monster said something awful to our youngest child, and I could take it no more.

I *yelled*.

I told him he was not to speak to our children that way. I told him he was a monster and that this was over. He screamed so violently that our child—our youngest, who has a Sensory Processing Disorder—grabbed their ears and burst into tears. The monster spewed hateful words toward our nine-year-old, deliberately blaming them for breaking up our family.

When we got home, I grabbed our children, threw them into the house for safety, and shut the door behind me. The monster thrust the door open, screamed, "Fuck you! We're done!" and threw his ring so hard it hit my face and chipped a glass left on the coffee table as it fell to the ground.

The children were shaking. He drove out of our driveway. I stayed awake with them for hours, praying with them, singing to them, and calming their fears.

He didn't come back that night. He was gone the entirety of the next day. There was so much peace in the immediate household, but severe paranoia and anxiety rushed through my veins.

I was notified of a purchase on our shared iCloud account.

Tinder.

I laughed and laughed and laughed a little more. It really *was* ending. With the sunshine on my back porch looking over acre upon acre, mile upon mile of the foothill landscape that he had tried to—yet again—ensnare me in, I was feeling unmeasurable joy. I made dinner for the children, read to them, kissed them goodnight, and went to sleep with hope in my heart.

20

"Breathe, darling. You survived before, and you'll do it again."

— MAXWELL DIAWUOH

THIS CHAPTER WILL BE BRIEF, AS I WILL UTILIZE IT AS A WARNING —a safe place for you to rest before we get to the hard part. I want you to understand that you're still allowed to read on if your life isn't filled with abusive people (be they parents, partners, or even bosses). You are still welcome here because this information is important. There are people in this world who need you to believe them. Who need you to speak up for them. Who need you to step outside your comfort zone and step in to save theirs. You might not be able to relate to my words, but someone in your life can. I hope I've given you the courage to leap, even if you fear losing your friend forever. If you're wrong, and your friend is just fine, I promise they won't be angry with you (and if they are, they weren't really your friend, were they?). But if you're right, you've saved their emotional/mental well-being, if not their life.

For those of you beautiful humans who are dealing with an

abusive situation right now or who have in the past and are still healing... guys, I see you. I feel you. I AM you. This book has not been easy to write. This has torn my heart open and made me re-live a bunch of things I was hoping to forget. But you know what it's also done? Spread a big ol' spotlight on a life that almost went silent at the hands of her abuser.

I don't want your voice to disappear. I don't want your families to miss you and suffer with the guilt that they should have said something when they had the chance. Please take this book and hold it up like a shield. It's time to get out of the situation you are in. Staying for the kids or financial ease is NOT okay. You need to show your children that being treated this way isn't love. Because friends... It's not love. Pack your bags, grab your kids, and get to safety. You WILL survive, you WILL thrive, and you WILL have the life you deserve. Is it going to be easy? Absolutely not! But is your life easy now? No, absolutely not. Resources are available to you—some are fantastic, and some require a little work.

My point is—you can do this.

If you are a man reading this, do not think for one second I'm not preaching to you, too. At the end of this book, I promise I will address just how abused you are and how our society does NOTHING to stop it. I see you, too.

Now, my wonderful friends... I love you. Know this right here, and right now, I am okay. I am a survivor—not a victim. My entire life today is like living in a dang fairytale, and I cannot wait to tell you about it sometime soon. There is hope, there is rest, and there is promise in life after abuse.

Your phoenix just has to rise from the ashes, first.

Now, this goes without saying:

THE FOLLOWING CHAPTER IS FILLED WITH A HORRIFIC AND VIOLENT RETELLING OF A REAL-LIFE SITUATION.

IF YOU NEED TO TAKE A BREAK, PLEASE DO SO.

UNDERSTAND THAT SOME OF THE DESCRIPTIONS MAY NOT BE 100% ACCURATE, AS THEY ARE BEING TOLD FROM MEMORY, AND MY MEMORY OF THIS MOMENT IN TIME IS UNDERSTANDABLY BRUISED.

IT IS ON COURT RECORD. IF YOU MUST, GET THE LEGAL DETAILS OF THE CASE.

BE PATIENT WITH YOURSELF. BE KIND AND LOVING TO YOURSELF.

YOU ARE LOVED. YOU ARE NEEDED. YOU ARE SEEN.

21

"Oh, how your kingdom will fall... When you find that your discarded pawn was the queen all along."

— *ERIN VAN VUREN*

THE NEXT MORNING, MY MONSTER CAME HOME. *EARLY.* WE'RE talking 0700 hours. He declared he was taking the kids to school and would be home soon after so we could talk. I couldn't argue. I could only pray that he wasn't kidnapping our children or that this would be the last time I'd see them alive. I told our oldest I would see them at their cross-country meet. I told them both how much I loved them... just in case. It was a sickening feeling —one that still makes my stomach churn.

I watched the three of them drive away in the only car I could drive (which meant I couldn't escape), and I immediately texted all that knew about my situation that my monster had returned and, if they didn't hear from me soon, to alert the police.

I was praying aloud as I nervously gathered things around the house. I wasn't sure what was about to happen, but I was aggravated that my pajama shorts didn't have pockets so I could keep my phone close and out of his sight. I grabbed my car keys, put them under my pillow, and turned my phone silent. I had never felt more unprepared in my life.

When he returned, he was unnervingly calm. He smelled like he'd just walked out of the shower, and his clothes were clean. Those two facts stood out, but I couldn't focus on them for long. He instructed me to go to our bedroom so that we could talk. That was the *last* place I wanted to be, but he made it clear I was not to argue. I knew my phone and keys were there, though, so I obliged.

He began by telling me that he had spent the previous 36 hours doing a lot of thinking. We talked for two hours, and I believe he thought it was enough to save our marriage. It wasn't. Though, at one point in our ghastly long conversation, I had a fleeting moment where I wanted to kiss him. I believe to this day that it was a surge of who he'd trained me to be—the last remnants of the hollow shell of who I was no longer allowing myself to be trying to surface one last time. But I threw her back in her cage and focused on my newfound strength. I left his words hanging in the air, thick like the smoke we'd been choking on all summer:

"Please, *please* stay. I'm sorry."

I took the opportunity to ask about the purchase he'd made the day before. I asked if he was already talking to other women. He told me he was. Three women, in fact. The anger welled up and overflowed. I finally began to cry—but not because I was hurt. I cried because I finally saw with the clearest of eyes what a fool I was. I had held on for so long, remaining faithful to a man who had no qualms about moving on the moment he felt rejected. And for all I knew, this wasn't the first time he had done something like this. I believe he was careless on purpose, but all the years prior? Who knows what/who he had done.

I wonder now if I had done the same all those years earlier, instead of grabbing that damn book... no, I'd be dead. There was no way I could lie about being with someone else while being married to him. He would have found out, and he would have killed me.

I demanded to see the women's profiles. I wanted to see the lies he was spewing. The women were ten times more beautiful than me, and it hurt because I saw what the years of fear, anguish, and abuse had done to my body... to my face.

My anger did not protect me like my irreverence did until that point.

I grabbed my keys and tried to rush past him.

He wouldn't let me leave our room. He blocked me from the door, not letting me pass. When I attempted to get by again, he grabbed me by the waist, picked me up, and threw me on the bed like you might toss a sock that you found on the floor. He told me to stay, just like you would a dog, and I... the brave and perhaps stupid girl that I was, said the one word that was always guaranteed to light a fire in my monster's belly.

"No."

That was the beginning of the three-and-a-half-hour fight for my life.

My years of premonitions and nightmares were coming true as my monster unleashed hell on me. The amount of pain and unequivocal fear my body endured was something I would not wish on anyone. He wouldn't allow me to leave. He thrashed and threw my body around the house like a rice-filled sock. He removed my insulin pump from my body because it was "in the way." He pushed me against the walls, breaking a picture frame over my head. My poor dog was barking and trying to help me as much as she could. He kicked her in the face after he threw me over the couch. Her yelp and the look of sheer devastation in her eyes were enough to give me some strength. I jumped up and bolted for the door before he could grab me. I was able to get outside. I ran screaming for the closest neighbor's house, but he went out the back door, cornered me by the side of our home, picked me up, and threw me over his shoulder caveman-style while I screamed.

The dutiful, *godly* man.

In the course of those three and a half hours, I was able to convince him I needed to use the restroom. It was the strangest break in his madness—a gift from someone above, in the end. He let me go but said he was timing me. He didn't know it, but I'd managed to steal my phone from the couch where it had fallen out of his pocket. He'd found it earlier and taken it and my car keys, "Just in case."

I ran to the bathroom and texted my father and stepmother.

Help. He's back. He's hurting me. Call the police. I love you.

Send.

Immediately, I realized what would happen if my monster found out I'd not only taken my phone but what he'd do if he discovered I cried for help.

Delete.

Do messages even go through if you delete them before they're sent?

I panicked.

Snapchat!

It was an app I wasn't allowed to have. But I had it. I loved playing with our children using the funny filters and taking pictures together. I knew one thing about it: direct messages disappeared after they were seen.

Help. He's back. He's hurting me. Call the police.

I sent a message to a guy I'd only just met. A man who lived across the country—but since he was the only one on Snapchat

I could see was available at that time, I took a risk. I didn't care that we barely knew each other.

Send.

Pray.

BANG! BANG!

My monster was at the door. My time was up. He found me with my phone. He was so furious he tore my shirt from the bottom to the collar to expose my breasts. He shoved his fingers deep inside me. I screamed in pain, and he got hard. "Ohhhoho! Look at this! She's ready for me, isn't she? Of course, she is because she likes to be taken advantage of. She likes it when her *Master* takes what's his. She likes to get hurt because she's a FUCKING WHORE!"

He became so excited his crazed eyes glazed over in euphoria. He shoved me to the ground, grabbed the back of my head, and tried to force himself into my mouth. I slapped his erection out of my face, the force sending him to his knees. I tried to escape again, but he was at the door before I could get there. He pulled me back to our room and slammed me on the bed again in a swift WWE maneuver. This time, he was completely naked.

I was done for.

He mounted me while simultaneously squeezing the air from my lungs with his Hulk-strength legs. This was the moment I distinctly remember wishing I had taken Jiu-Jitsu after all; at least I would have had a sliver of a chance to survive this. I was starting to see white spots appear in my eyes from a lack of oxygen. I knew I needed to get my body a little more upright to breathe. I pulled myself onto my elbows and screamed until my voice box gave out.

"Please stop. PLEASE," was all I could say in a raspy plea. Tears were cascading from my eyes. I was certain he'd cracked or broken my ribs. I was certain I was going to die.

He pushed my forehead, which knocked me off my elbows.

Those white spots in my eyes had returned. In fact, they were starting to twinkle.

"No! This is what you wanted, isn't it? YOU wanted THIS!"

Pain shot through me. I blacked out and can only assume he was violating me. I came to but couldn't feel below the waist. Something heavy hit my head... his duty belt—complete with his taser *and* gun—and it was within reach, just above me. The thought crossed my mind: *Can I really shoot this man? Can I really take a human life? Our kids will be left with no one.*

He must have read my mind because he let out the most jovial chuckle.

"Oh, you're a mischievous little thing, aren't you? Let's take *that* temptation away, shall we? But thanks for reminding me... we must do something with those hands of yours. They're a little too... free."

I couldn't even scream anymore. I'd screamed for three hours straight. I was cuffed to the bed, and he was squeezing the air from my lungs. He put a ball gag in my mouth so tightly that the corners of my mouth were bleeding.

This was it.

I kept thinking about our children. I focused on their laughs, on their smiles, and the moment each of them called me *Momma* for the first time. I looked into their eyes, those memories I had stored for a lifetime. They were going to be orphans because there was no way this man was going to kill me and make it out alive.

I couldn't die, not like this. They needed me. I needed to be at that cross-country meet. They were counting on me.

God, WHERE ARE YOU?!! My babies need me!

I felt my forehead pulsating with each ever-slowing heart-beat. My blood pressure was high, but my heart was slow—I'm not sure how else to explain it. My vision was growing blurry and dim. My body was giving out. He was winning. I was fading. I wasn't going to survive. Was I supposed to make peace here? Was I supposed to give up and let it go?

I was tired. I was so, so tired.

I whispered my children's names, hoping they could hear me in their hearts at that moment. I told them I loved them. I told them I would always be with them, no matter where they'd go. I said I was sorry. I said I tried my best. I told them not to be like me.

"I love you, babies—"

BANG, BANG, BANG!

Our front door.

Someone was at the freaking front door.

He looked at me in shock, releasing my airway. His personal cell phone rang. Then, his work cell phone.

"Well, this is it, baby. They've come to get me. It's been a good time."

He uncuffed me just enough that I had to release myself the rest of the way, just as he'd taught me to if I ever got kidnapped for being a Federal Law Enforcement Officer's wife.

I heard him open the front door to one of his best friends from another agency in full uniform and gun unholstered a bit (as I found out later). My monster was stark naked. I was screaming in the bedroom. I heard some shuffling of feet—I assumed they were throwing clothes on him. Then I heard that sound, that blessed sound that I had longed to hear:

Click, click.

My monster was in police custody.

As the officer, our family friend, called out to me that it was safe, I released my bonds and gag and ran to him, sobbing. He met me in our bedroom. I collapsed in his arms. He stroked my hair and helped keep my shirt together.

"Hey, hey... shhh. It's okay, Bethany. We got him. Shhh... I'm so sorry. We got him. We got him. Did he do this? Shit. Can I get you another shirt?"

My monster was in the back of a police car. Detectives and the crime scene unit were called.

My nightmare was over.

22

"Eventually, he will only be a memory of what you didn't want from love."

— *MARK ANTHONY*

As a society, we don't really think about what happens next, do we? When a life has been shattered, we don't realize that it has to somehow be put back together. My first, most important step when my monster was taken away was getting to my children. My oldest had their final cross-country meet that day, so I would pick my youngest up early, grab some road trip snacks, and head to the school over 40 minutes away. But by the time the Crime Scene Unit arrived, I realized I was going to miss the meet.

My heart was shattered.

I called the school and told them we had a major emergency and that I needed my youngest to ride the bus home. I explained that my oldest would have to get a ride in the school van after the meet, and I would pick them up when they arrived.

I felt like the worst mom on the planet. I knew I had let them down, and that made me cry harder.

Funny thing, shock. Shock made me do and feel a lot of strange things in those first two hours. I started cleaning the house. I was so humiliated to have all these people go through the messy house because of the struggle. I tried to clean the shattered glass on the floor; I tried to start the laundry. The detectives demanded I stop because everything was evidence. They wouldn't allow me to return to my room, as that was the primary crime scene.

With wobbly knees, I made it to my dining room table and sat with detectives. I explained what happened. I told them everything, but my head was spinning, and my blood sugar was high. Remember, that monster removed my insulin pump from my body hours earlier. I am a Type 1 Diabetic, and I needed insulin immediately, but my brain couldn't explain that to the detectives. When one of them asked me about the medical port on my side, that's when I remembered. His eyes widened when I asked if I could get my pump from my nightstand.

He nodded but then stopped me. He asked the crime scene photographer to take a picture of my nightstand and then allowed me to retrieve it.

Sitting back down, I continued my story.

The front door swung open, and there stood my little one. My nine-year-old was staring right at me with eyes as wide as the universe.

"Mom? Mom?? MOM!"

They ran to my arms. They were sobbing. I was sobbing.

"What is going on? Why are all the police here? Did Daddy do something to you?"

Ladies and gentlemen, to try and explain the emotions that coursed through my body at hearing that final question is impossible. I knew my child knew. They were scared this would happen when the monster started screaming about this entire thing being *their* fault for speaking about how they felt.

I wanted to protect my child with a lie but free them with the truth.

I said, "I'm okay. We're going to be okay. But your dad made a really bad mistake, and he hurt me. I don't think you'll see him for a while."

My sweet second-born looked me dead in the eyes and said, "Okay. Good."

I held them so tight.

One of the female officers asked if she could take my baby out for a walk. They protested a bit, but I promised I wasn't going anywhere.

The entire house was filled with cops. Many of them shook their heads, uncomfortable that one of their own had done this. So many times, I heard how sloppy that monster was with his equipment; stray bullets were always lying around the house, and his duty belt (as mentioned before) was carelessly thrown onto the bed. His uniforms were tossed about, his gun cabinet was not locked, and no key could be found.

That was my life: reckless, careless, ridiculous.

"I'm just consistently inconsistent, baby. That's me. You get what you get, and you'll like it that way."

Words I heard so often, I knew that one day I would write a book and title it that.

Here we are.

It'd been nearly four hours when the detectives suggested I grab my things and figure out a different place to stay for a little while. They arrested him on hefty charges but could never guarantee that someone like him wouldn't make bail. I called a friend that my monster had allowed me to interact with from time to time—a friend who had a bad feeling and tried to call me while my monster and I were talking (I still have the voice-mail on my phone to this day because it meant so much to me that she'd try and check-in)—and told her what happened. She freaked out and immediately jumped in to help. She offered to meet me at the hospital to take the kids and the dog. She would feed them dinner and transport them all to my father.

My father.

Oh, my dad. That man didn't know what to do. I still have his voicemail from that day, too, on my phone. As it turned out, the message I'd sent him and his wife *had* gone through. The voice-mails from both of them are haunting. My stepmother was panicked but tried to keep a neutral voice. My father sounded like his world had shattered. I didn't believe I was that important to him until that moment. When I called him, he was stifling tears. He had a million questions, but I couldn't answer them. I told him how I needed help, and he didn't hesitate.

The detectives said I needed to get going. I had to pick up my oldest from the school and get to the hospital to do my evalua-tion and rape kit.

When I pulled into the school, a nice woman was waiting with my oldest. They had been there for a little too long, and my worried little one was not handling it well. The detective escorting me to the hospital drove in first and then let me drive in. When I saw my brave kiddo, they ran straight to the car and into my arms.

"Mom! What happened? What is going on? Why is there an unmarked car with you? Why weren't you there? I did a good job, but I needed you."

Oh, friends. The weight on my heart was almost unbearable.

On the 45-minute drive to the hospital, I went into a little more detail with both of my children. I did not mention vivid details, mind you; I simply told them that their father hurt me really badly, that he was arrested, and that I wasn't sure we would see him for a while.

"Are you guys going to get a divorce, Mommy?" My oldest child wasn't taking this information well. Missing half of their temporal lobe meant missing the ability to connect emotions to situations they are in. That was not going to make any of this easy.

"Yes, love. Yes. No one should live with someone who hurts them like this."

My youngest sighed in relief. "Good."

I told them what was about to happen and said they weren't going to go back to school for the week. I told them I had no clue what each hour would look like, but I swore I would keep them safe.

I arrived at the hospital where my friend was waiting. Guys, everyone needs a friend in their life like Bridgette. I didn't have to ask for or explain anything. She asked me if I had enough gas to get where I needed to go. I didn't, but I had no clue where my wallet was in all this mess. A new wave of panic pulsed through me. She handed me her credit card and didn't say a word. She hugged me and said that I was free, that I was safe, and that she "was gonna kill that bastard."

The detective was standing with me at that point, and he chuckled. Bridgette laughed and apologized, but the detective shook his head.

"Nah, we all feel that way right now. He's not making it out of this, don't you worry."

I hugged my babies. I hugged my dog. I hugged Bridgette—my sweet savior of the moment. She was the angel I needed, and her lack of hesitation made me feel so secure.

The detective and I went inside and had to wait for a while. I had to shut my phone off because my monster's arrest had made the news, mugshot and all. I was getting so many texts and DMs I couldn't even check the time accurately. In my nervousness, I tried to break the awkward silence with 82,000 questions. My first and most important question was probably the one you're asking yourself: How did the cops find out?

"It's crazy, actually," the detective said. "You have some people who really care about you. Some woman called us for an immediate welfare check. She was from [another] county but didn't have your exact address. Apparently, you sent out something on Snapchat? And whoever you sent that out to sent her a message with a picture of the map where you lived. They're the ones who saved you."

The man across the country messaged my friend Audra. She was there with me when we met him a couple of weeks earlier at my family's event, where we had hired his band to play. So, she was at least somewhat familiar with him. He messaged her and told her to call the police.

It turns out he went on Facebook and found anyone and everyone I was related to and messaged them simultaneously. Bridgette, my father, and my brother later explained they'd received messages but thought they were a scam.

Audra, my very best friend (though I'd only spent time with her in person twice in the five years I'd known her), sprang into action. She'd known my monster and his family from a young age and felt uneasy about him. She called the police from work and did not give up harassing them until she knew I was safe.

Because of her and this man I'd met very briefly, I am alive today.

I asked the detective if he thought my monster would be released that night.

"Ohhhh no," he chuckled. "That man is facing several felonies, ma'am. His bail is currently set at nearly $1 million."

I remember looking down at my knee and zoning out for just a second. A bruise started forming on it from when he shoved me to the ground, but I felt no pain. He was going to be in jail for a while. This was real life. This was serious. I was finally on my own.

"Want something that will make you laugh a little?"

"Of course," I smiled, thankful for this man who was so wildly uncomfortable but knew how important his job was.

"Apparently, when they went to book him, he put up a fight saying he was some MMA fighter or some shit. The guards laughed at him. I guess one of them trained with him at their Jiu-Jitsu gym. Either way, that fool is sitting pretty... all on his own. Can't keep him with the regular crowd because he probably put a few of them in there."

I laughed. I laughed hysterically. It felt so good to laugh.

Okay, God. Thanks for that one.

I got checked out by an all-female group of doctors and nurses. They said I was a bit torn up internally, but otherwise, okay. Before I left, I had three missed calls from Victim's Services, offering support and giving me case information.

I was free to go.

I got in my car.

I buckled my seatbelt.

It began to rain.

I took off my wedding rings and placed them in my cup holder.

I turned on my car and pressed play on a Spotify playlist I'd never touched.

The beginning of "Alone In A Room—Acoustic Version" by my favorite band, Asking Alexandria, came on.

Admittedly, I hadn't heard it since its release earlier that summer. But I'm a sucker for lyrics. And those lyrics rang through me like a missing piece of my DNA. I played it again, aware that my life had finally changed.

I put my car in reverse, drove to a gas station, and, thanks to Bridgette—filled up.

I got on the freeway...

And smiled.

23

"She would walk barefoot through hell if that's what it would take for her to find her heart and soul again."

— *REGGIE NULAN*

FROM WHAT MOST OF US HAVE SEEN ON TELEVISION OR IN MOVIES, I wouldn't blame you one bit if, after an event like mine, you assumed I had thousands of offers of help—that the people in my life jumped in to save us, that the church I went to provided phone calls, shelter, or even love for my children and me. But that's not quite how it worked.

My father and stepmother took us in, our dog and all. They didn't hesitate, even though I knew they were uncomfortable. Having young children in the house where you were used to living your life uninterrupted and how you like it could not have been easy. Their house was massive, prim, and proper, like a museum. They sacrificed a lot to bring us there. I didn't know how, but I hoped it was only temporary.

I was abandoned by the church we attended at the time— immediately unfriended and unfollowed by people in the congregation whom I'd connected with on social media. That shocked me and showed me that humans aren't what makes a church. In fact, in the years since, I can count on one hand how many times I've stepped foot *in* a church building after making that discovery.

God and I... we have an understanding. I can't be around "His" people for long periods anymore. Most, not all, seem to have an agenda that I refuse to stand behind, and do not follow Christ's example of loving one another in any way. Now, I choose my path and don't feel the need to explain it to anyone because it's no one's business. I'm learning that boundaries are necessary, especially in a world that believes we all have the right to one another's religious or political affiliations.

I have wounds there that will never heal, but I will learn how to walk with them. I love to be out in nature, where my spirit can be quiet and my thoughts can slow down. For now, that's the gift of peace I have needed and so happily accept.

I was disregarded by that tiny foothill community I never fit into. Living in such a small town meant *everyone* knew what happened. When I came to the children's school to get transfer papers and the items from their desks, I was never looked at in the eyes. I was treated like a leper who may or may not infect the entire campus. Watching the kids say goodbye to yet another set of good friends ripped my soul from my body.

We were officially moving to my father's house, as I could not afford to stay where we were. I had separated all the contents of my home by what was mine and what was his. I was required to hand over his badges and uniforms to his captain, but everything else was fair game. Because I didn't know how the rules of divorce worked and was uncertain how long he'd be in jail, I bagged up everything of his and left it for his family to come and get. I cared nothing for the television, our wedding pictures, his notes to me over the years, or all my "law enforcement officer wife" shirts. I gave him everything, including his treasure box of torture, where he kept all the toys and devices he used against me, even the "award" and "punishment" boxes where I would have to pick what happened to me based on my behavior that day (hint: in all those years, I only got the "award" box once). And the rest, I put out for an estate sale.

I will never forget the people that came and bought items. As someone closed their car door, I heard through my open living room window, "No, I just want to see what she looks like..." I was on display for the entire rotten town.

A freakshow. Of course, I was.

I faced many angry calls—people filled to the brim with outrage because I had never informed them about what was going on behind closed doors as if they had the right to know. I even had one lady go as far as to say, "I let my daughters be around you and that man in your home. How could you not be honest? How could you put *my* children in danger?"

I found myself having to block many people in my life who I had thought were friends. That added a copious amount of pain to my already-broken heart. Not only was I struggling to figure out who I was, where my next meal was coming from, and how to file a billion pieces of paperwork to prevent that man from ever seeing me or my children again, but I also had to fight against humans who were mad at me for... daring to not trust them with my walking, breathing, and most terrifying fear?

It was nothing less than stark, raving insanity.

Not surprisingly, no one from my monster's family reached out to me. Not once. Save one phone call and a couple of texts from his grandmother, someone I loved and adored, asking to see the children. The phone call was short because I lost cell service while she was talking. She was awkward and hesitant. I got the impression she did not have the best of intentions. She asked how I could "do this" to her grandson in her text messages. Needless to say, I did not respond. As much as it breaks my heart, I had to block her, too.

But his parents never called. His brother and sister-in-law came straight to the house to take everything they could, including my second vehicle, without my consent or knowledge. It hadn't even been 24 hours since his arrest when they came and stole the car. I had spent so many years loving these people without being loved back. My brother-in-law's wife not reaching out is still a gaping wound I don't believe I will ever be able to mend.

I was overwhelmed by the negativity thrown in my direction. I couldn't imagine why I was being treated like a monster when I had done nothing more than survive a horrific incident. I was hurt by the silence from others, too. But I understood *them*. What could be said? Had they contributed to or not prevented my abuse over the years?

To those individuals, I must say this: I love you. You contributed nothing, and there was no way you could have known. That's how these situations work, guys. Victims become experts at hiding, faking that life is perfect, and *believing* that life is perfect. We wear impenetrable masks laced with explosives, so we do not dare let our guard down. We don't let you see. We don't. Do not blame yourselves.

To those who lashed out in anger, I have to say, though I will forever be confused by your reactions, I forgive you. I hope you have learned a valuable lesson that will result in you going out of your way to help someone in need. But mostly, I pray you are never in a situation like mine. I pray you are not abandoned by those you love. And I hope you are at peace within yourselves.

But then...

There were many, many people who *did* help.

Goodness, I could write an entire chapter with just their names. I was sent care packages, financial gifts, clothes for the children, wine, and bubble bath necessities for me. That first month alone, I had no money, no credit, no childcare (so no job), and I couldn't fathom how a 33-year-old human being couldn't stand alone on their own two feet.

I had people step in before I knew how to ask the right questions. My friend Audra hooked me up with a temp agency, where I was able to get a short-term job that aided in getting me enough gas money to drive to work and the offices for EBT assistance. My father and stepmother did what they could, but I was tired of depending on someone else. And my abused brain didn't trust them. I didn't trust anyone when they offered help. I felt like a burden. I felt like the waste of space I'd been told for years that I was.

When I had to borrow money, I hated myself. I had no real way to repay it, but I tried my best. I got just under $900 per month of cash assistance and $600 a month for food. I had two rapidly growing children who were always hungry. They were welcome but not welcome to eat my father's food. The children started getting passive-aggressive comments about how expensive my father's electricity bill was, and that stunned me with fear, leaving me frozen and incapable of feeling safe. So, I stopped eating meals three days a week for a little while. It helped keep our grocery bills down and devoted to the children.

"That's what mommas do, Bethie—they put their children first. Everything will work out, you'll see."

My mother's words echoed loudest in my ears to combat the growling of my hungry stomach.

You're right; thanks, Mom.

Before I could blink, Thanksgiving arrived, and my father's entire side of the family came to celebrate. I couldn't help but feel uncomfortable the whole time. No one knew what to say. How do they address the big, giant, bright pink Godzilla in the room? They didn't. At least most of them didn't. I needed to be surrounded, and I needed to be told they were happy I was alive. I needed to be reminded that they weren't going to abandon me. Those conversations didn't happen. Could I honestly blame them? My beautiful aunt (who is closer in age to be more like my big sister) was the only one to look me in the eyes that entire weekend. She kept me breathing, and I am grateful to her.

Christmas came—a time when magic happens. When you're surrounded by those you love, who embrace you, who bring out the best in you, but my children and I spent the entire day alone. Our first Christmas out of chaos, and we were alone. My father didn't cancel his trip and stay with his daughter and grandchildren on what was possibly the hardest day imaginable for them. But you know what I chose to see instead? The dozens of gifts that people—some who were complete strangers—sent to my children. The tree that stood, with lights and ornaments, all brand new out of the packages, was paid for by a high school friend and her girlfriend, whom I'd run into at Walmart just the week before. I was just excited to see them and get hugs. But when they threw a gift card into my cart as they walked by before I left, I didn't know what to do. Several acts of pure love changed the course of my entire holiday.

I know it sounds like the aftermath was all just more negativity, but it wasn't. It was hard to count blessings in those days, but the ones I remember vividly are the things I think back on when times get tough. I had a beautiful roof over my head and a bed to sleep in. I was in the room my Nana had passed away in. I felt her peace each and every day. I probably spent more hours there than I had anywhere else in years. My children were safe and, most importantly, comfortable telling me their thoughts and feelings. I was thankful for the people who checked in on me, who asked nothing of me other than to know how I was doing. I was thankful for the Facebook people who supported my children by helping them get to camp or contributed to fundraisers. All in all, I truly found out who my tribe was.

Did it hurt in some areas? It sure did! In the end, was I able to surround myself with humans I could trust, being all the wiser for the future? Yes, yes indeed.

I was working side-by-side with a lawyer to get my divorce finalized. The lawyer was given to me by Victim's Services, and they aided with court details, filed documents, and made phone calls on my behalf; there were many things I could not do. They were beacons of light on the darkest days. I had to face my monster in court 28 days after the arrest. For some reason, the paperwork had been mixed up when I filed for a restraining order, and the courts believed I was filing for custody of our children. Admittedly, I filled all the paperwork out myself the day after the arrest, so I'm sure my shaky hands checked off the wrong boxes a few times. The judge granted my restraining order but did not grant me sole custody until he could better understand what the criminal court was planning to do.

I know. Believe me, I know.

None of that made any sense.

The District Attorney was in touch with me, too. Constantly. She was young and detested cases like mine. She was angry and wanted justice. In the end, she went after four felonies. He and his court-appointed lawyer denied it all. Then they saw that the DA wasn't going to budge. Eventually, at the six-month mark, the court was set up, and I had to testify to bring our case to trial.

But let me interrupt this part of the story to tell you about my friend Natalie.

Natalie is a friend I have known since my freshman year of high school. We've stayed in touch over the years—she has been ever-present at every huge milestone in my life. Just after that fateful day, Natalie was the first to do what she could to visit my children and me. She gave the children gifts, took us to dinner, and vowed never to let anyone hurt us again. I believed her. But one of the things she brought up when I was talking to her about the trial was my monster had removed my insulin pump. With a puzzled, determined look, she asked, "Did you tell the DA about this detail? Because Beth… that's attempted murder."

I hadn't thought of that.

The day I was brought in to testify, I sat in a waiting room for a very, very long time. I was scared out of my mind. I had already faced my monster twice in open court because of the custody issue. He behaved like a fool both times, telling the judge I was cheating on him and that he was a good *Christian* man. It was horrifying.

But this time, I had to speak. This time, I had to re-live what had happened. The same detectives who interviewed me on that horrific day were there. They came in to give me a reassuring hug. I made mention of the insulin pump and asked if that was in their report. One said it was, but it was a minor detail. I explained how it *wasn't* a minor detail and reminded him there was a picture of my pump on my nightstand. His eyes lit up. He did not even excuse himself—he left the room without a word. The DA called me into the courtroom. I kept my head facing forward but could not lift my eyes. I didn't want to see him. The blood was so hot in my hands, down my spine, and in my face. I heard Natalie's voice in the back of my mind, "*He* did this, love. It's time he rots in hell."

I looked up.

My monster was sitting there, having gained at least 25 pounds since I last saw him. He'd shaved his head, undoubtedly (knowing him) to make him seem tougher. He was shaking his head as his right leg bounced in rage. I was terrified but had to keep going. This was for my babies. This was for ME.

I stood in the aisle after the DA stopped me. The court-appointed attorney interrupted us by saying he was no longer prepared and requesting a new date. My monster shouted, "This is BULLSHIT!"

Apparently, the new evidence brought forth that day changed things a bit.

The DA hugged me after I was escorted out of the room. She called me brilliant for bringing up the insulin pump and said she'd let me know if she needed me anytime soon. I hugged her back and said, "Don't thank me. My friend Natalie was the brains behind this." I turned around to the faces of the two detectives. They congratulated me, and one of them whispered, "To Natalie!"

Our family friend, the first officer on the scene, the one I will always hold as my personal angel, stood behind the crowd surrounding me. He was leaning against the railing, arms crossed, slightly shaking his head. I moved through the detectives toward him. I hugged him so tight—the memory of the last time I hugged him flashed through my mind: My shirt was torn from the bottom all the way to the collar, my wrists were in excruciating pain from the handcuffs, and my lips were cracked and bleeding. Then, I hugged him because I was grasping for safety. This time, I hugged him to assure him I was safe. He had tears in his eyes and was apologizing all over again. He told me he was proud of me, and that I was not alone. "If you ever need anything, remember that [my wife] and I are always here for you."

Less than six months later, my monster took a plea deal. He would serve a 20-year sentence for the following felonies:

- Corporal injury of spouse
- False imprisonment by violence
- Sexual penetration by foreign object with force and violence
- Rape of spouse by force/fear/threat

- Attempted murder

To Natalie.

I did not have to endure a trial. I wrote a letter to the judge for sentencing and included letters that both my children requested to be read. I have no idea if any of the letters were read, but if they were, I cannot fathom what that monster's reaction was.

In the end, it doesn't matter how he felt or what he heard. What matters is that I was free to raise my children. I could watch them grow up free from fear, free from the delusion that women are unimportant, free from the idea that being gay is a disgrace to humanity, free from believing different races had to stay in their own lanes, free from walking on eggshells, free from believing their worth was only held in their father's approval.

Free. We were free.

24

"The ghosts of all the women you used to be are all so proud of who you have become, storm child made of wild and flame."

— *NIKITA GILL*

FRIENDS, YOU HAVE JOURNEYED WITH ME THROUGH SOME OF MY life's most painful moments. Granted, this is a small snippet of the whole package deal. There were plenty of happy moments during that time that did not fit the narrative of this memoir. Understand that my monster had good in him, or else I wouldn't have gotten two *incredible* human beings out of the marriage. On his good days, he would sing. On his good days, he had jokes and a laugh that made me laugh harder. He took me to a famous theme park for our 10th wedding anniversary. He insisted we had matching shirts, and he even got down on one knee to reclaim his love for me with a ring to mark the occasion. He had those rare moments that kept convincing me I was insane for always being afraid.

But even those happy memories are scarred with dark moments that left me trembling.

That's abuse.

That's what it feels like to believe *you* are the crazy one.

As a society, we are learning new terms every day—ones like gaslighting, narcissistic abuse, and trauma response. I don't know that we have them all 100% accurate by definition because we are now quick to label every negative interaction with a term that closely resembles how we feel. But understand this: if you are not feeling SAFE or feeling like you can change your life without threat of harm, then you must get help.

I learned a lot about programs like Victim's Services, and as much as they try to help, they can't always get it right. So, if you need help, acquire as much of it as possible until you are safe.

Mental, emotional, and verbal abuse is—IS!!!—abuse. You can and should get help. You are so important; you do not deserve to be told otherwise. You are allowed to be YOU, no matter what that looks like. And if there are humans in your life who are extinguishing your flame, it's time you gather the power within you and get out.

But, Bethany... they will kill me.

I hear you. I hear you. I hear you. If that is the case, then your escape is not as conventional as I'm making it sound. It's not the pack-your-bags-and-get-out-of-town kind of situation. It will take a coordinated effort. Start by talking to someone you trust. Give yourself a date and a time when you will flee. If you are in the United States, call the **National Domestic Violence Hotline** at **(800) 799-7233** or text "**START**" to **88788**. If you are outside the USA, there are websites that will help you find the numbers you need. Go to **thehotline.org**, which has an immediate escape button and ways to clear your browser in an emergency.

But, Bethany... I feel I will be judged just like you were. I cannot handle that kind of loss.

Oh, friend. I know. It's not easy at all. A close friend of mine stood up to her abuser, and no one outside her family believed her. She had pictures and evidence, but in the end, she's having to rebuild her life. I text her from time to time, offering support and a listening ear. I am always baffled by how deceitful her (now) ex-husband is and how he has convinced everyone that she was "crazy." She is one of the strongest women I know; her story will be one of sheer, guttural strength. She is my hero, and I cannot wait to see how she blossoms when the time is right.

Having that kind of loss after standing up for your own worth is painful. But are these people really worth your mental, emotional, and physical decline? Would you recommend that *anyone* in your situation do the same? Of course not. You will rise. You will have a life you are proud of with people who support and love you. These humans you're afraid of getting judged by? You'll forget their names. You will forget their faces. I promise you.

But, Bethany... I'm a man. My wife is conniving and cruel; she makes me question my sanity and constantly threatens to take our children from me. That's not abuse, is it?

Love, yes. Yes, it is abuse. You are a man... *and*? Are you not a human deserving of love, kindness, support, and care? Our society has failed you. Too often, movies, sitcoms, and social media videos depict men being abused as though it's some joke. How often do we see women slapping a man across the face for him saying something rude or offensive on our screens? I'm sorry, I hate to break it to you, but that's unwanted physical abuse. Joking that a man is stupid and cannot function without a woman's intelligence is *not* okay! Turn it around: Would those jokes or scenes be accepted the other way?

Men, I personally know a few of you who have been whittled away at the hands and words of a partner. You deserve to leave. You deserve love, sanity, and peace. You are not exempt from the notion that your existence freaking matters. If you are reading this book, I thank you. And I applaud you. I am here for you and am ready to fight this battle with you. Something in our society must change.

But, Bethany... I believe that wives need to submit to their husbands.
Doesn't that mean that I am required to do as he says?

<u>NO!!!</u>

I do not believe for one flipping second that that is what the apostle Paul meant in that overused, over-abused verse in the Bible. There are a million theories out there, but in no way do I believe that God allows men to treat their women however they deem fit. I am not a pastor, I do not have a degree in theology, and I certainly am not one to speak on behalf of *any* God. But to use *any* Bible (or whatever book your religion of choice looks to) verse as an excuse to harm, demean, humiliate, defile, or desecrate another human being is W-R-O-N-G!! Do not, and I repeat, do *not* argue with me or any abuse victim on this subject. Utilizing any god or religion to hurt someone else is not okay. EVER. Are you required to do what your husband says? Listen, I am not in your home, so I do not have the authority to answer that with precision. I *can* tell you that no one should force you to do something you do not want or are uncomfortable with.

But, Bethany... my children. I promised them our family would always stay together.

Boy, do I hear you on that one. My heart breaks with you because I never saw myself as a divorced woman. But just the other day, I overheard my second child (who is now 14) tell their friend, "Yeah, my parents divorced when I was younger. My mom saved us from my biological father. She's... my hero."

Friends, I promise you, teaching your children how *not* to be treated is worth so much more than the hassle of shared custody. Teaching those babies who look to you for guidance that you CAN and WILL succeed, even after the most terrible trials are over, is priceless. You are modeling self-respect, self-love, and self-honor. Staying just for them, despite the pain and anguish you suffered, will only give them a sensation of guilt they will never escape from.

But, Bethany... I love them. What if they change?

Again, I am not an expert in any of this. I am not a licensed therapist (yet!) and cannot give you "official" advice. Imagine we're at a coffee shop, and you ask me these things. I'll give you the advice, and you take what you want from it and apply it where you feel you need it. That being said, you love them. Well, yeah! Of course you do, friend. Am I saying the love of your life is incapable of change? Absolutely not. I always recommend communication, therapy sessions together and separately, and lots and lots of work. Anything is possible. You follow what works for you, but do not, I repeat, do *not* stay if you are being assaulted. Get the help you need before you can't.

Oh, how I wish I could be with all of you right now. How I wish we were sitting together, mulling over this whole book together—getting a better understanding of what it means and how to move on into the future: a safer, stronger, more beautiful future together. But you know what? I believe in you. And I know you are on this earth for a reason. I'm glad you are alive and are processing this life with open eyes. That's not easy to do, you know. But look at you... just sitting there making it all happen.

I am aware that I am a lucky case. Several people in my position have not been so lucky and have wound up with obliterated bodies and/or minds. Some have not made it out alive, having never escaped their abusive circumstances. I recognize and honor all those people with my words because they deserve to be seen. I also know that the justice my monster was served doesn't come swiftly or at all for other monsters, and some of you are having to deal with yours even though you aren't living with them any longer.

I cannot imagine how that feels.

There's freedom, but not really.

There's peace, but not really.

You are constantly reminded of your monster and are possibly still subjected to their poisonous words.

If that's your situation, I want you to find an accountability partner or several accountability partners. It's important to surround yourself with at least one person you know you can trust with every thought, every emotion, every fear, and every concern. Trust me, your therapist is awesome, and I hope you are getting great work done there. But I want you to find someone you can just... *be* around. Someone in your corner who wants to be there and does not have to be paid to do so. This person will not pass judgment when you call with sheer outrage spewing from your lungs after a passive-aggressive comment during a custody exchange. This person will snap you back into reality when you doubt your power and self-worth. This person (or persons!) will keep you going strong, with no agenda required.

As someone who is that for a few ladies I know currently in this situation, I promise you it is your friend's honor to stand in your corner. You are not now, nor ever have been, nor ever will be a burden to the people who genuinely love you.

25
———

"And here you are living despite it all."

— RUMI

As we bring this book to a close, I would like to offer a little hope.

I want to tell you, ever so carefully, what my life looks like now because I need you to see that the road to recovery and healing from major trauma is worth it.

Keep in mind, I am FAR from healed. I am incredibly uncomfortable being alone with men, even if I know them. I have discovered I have destructive nervous habits, such as scratching a little hole into the side of my thumb when I feel I am going to be, or am, in trouble (something I must have done most of my marriage). I am just now conquering my fear of looking men in the eye or lowering my head when they raise their voice. Healing takes time. No one knows the frustration of wanting to be "fine" more than me.

At the release of this memoir, I will be just shy of the 5th anniversary of that tragic day. My mother will have been gone for ten years, my sweet Nana for six, and my oldest child will be nine years seizure-free.

I have traveled to many places all over the United States, moved across the country, secured my own houses to rent, bought my own car, and worked as a paraprofessional for some of the most incredible high school and post-high school students, with whom I am still in contact today. I have been a writing teacher at a private school, which motivated me to do something I was told I could never do: go back to school and complete my degree in psychology with an emphasis on mental health. My plan when I graduate? To help those who have been abused and remove the stigma on all of us.

I am an editor working alongside one of my very best friends, someone who has helped me grow not only as a woman but as a friend. She has torn down some of my walls and has shown me what I am capable of. Being able to edit other writers' manuscripts and encourage them to pursue their dreams has been a gift all on its own. I love what I do and am thankful to have the opportunity.

I have watched my children grow exponentially (they are both towering over me now) and expand their minds, diving deeper into their own interests. My oldest is destined for a military career that will undoubtedly span the course of their life. My youngest already designs games that have been viewed and played by millions—yes, MILLIONS—all over the world. They are both wise, kind, and have no interest in the life they used to live. Their eyes are focused forward, with a love for all humans in their hearts. Both have decided to never have a drop of alcohol. Both are undecided about bringing children of their own into this world. They stand up for themselves and are major advocates for basic human rights. They are my heroes.

But perhaps my favorite news of all starts with a question:

Remember that man to whom I sent a message on

Snapchat? The one who did all he could to make sure the police got to me in time?

That man... is now my husband.

I told you, I live a fairytale life now. I have never known love, partnership, strength, and peace like I currently experience. He has walked with me through all these hardships, these victories, and every painstaking hour it has taken me to write this book. He is my rock, my beacon, and my mirror. He shows me my worth, and I, in turn, show him his. I have shared every single detail of my past, even when it was difficult. He has listened, counseled, and encouraged me to seek help whenever needed. We have consistently worked on trust, patiently helping one another understand each other on hard days. His past is awfully similar to mine, if not worse—spanning deeper into his childhood. Because of this, we actively work together to solidify our communication and strengthen our bond.

He also brought something incredible with him to our new life together. He brought another child for me to love. A child born in my heart, they are the essence of bravery, love, and kindness. I have never known a child with such tenacity and sincerity. I am thankful for the opportunity to be in their life and to watch all three children laugh and play together. Being a blended family has given us joy that cannot seem to be superseded by anything on this planet. We go on adventures together, experience new opportunities with one another, and challenge each other to achieve our dreams. I don't know how life could get any better. I love catching myself with a smile as I mutter my new mantra:

Wow, I can't believe it's this easy.

Redemption and second chances are real. Happiness is real. Healing is real. You simply have to be brave and step out of your current realm of chaos in order to find the places where they exist.

I challenge you now:

Get help.

Step in.

Speak up.

Show up.

Whatever the situation is, you are powerful enough to stop it. You are strong enough to fix it. You are brave enough to move past it.

I believe in you. I am proud of you. I am thankful for you, for your grace, for your existence.

I will leave you with the first poem I wrote—the first one in over a decade—written the day after I almost died. It's yours now, just like your life is.

Be encouraged and know that your journey... is not over.

> But I refuse.
> I refuse to sink.
> I refuse to believe that the phoenix within me
>   won't rise from the ashes you tried to bury
>   me in.

— BETHANY, 2018